THEN AND THERE SERIES
GENERAL EDITOR
MARJORIE REEVES, M.A., PH.D.

CW00690313

A Coal and Iron Community in the Industrial Revolution 1760–1860

JOHN ADDY

Illustrated from contemporary sources

LONGMAN

LONGMAN GROUP UK LIMITED
Longman House, Burnt Mill, Harlow,
Essex CM20 2JE, England
and Associated Companies throughout the World.

First published 1969
Ninth impression 1986

ISBN 0-582-20456-9

Produced by Longman Group (FE) Ltd
Printed in Hong Kong

ACKNOWLEDGEMENTS
For permission to reproduce photographs we are grateful to the following: Aerofilms, page 86; British Museum, pages 9, 22, 23, 61 *middle* and *below*, 99 *above* and *below*; Earl Fitzwilliam, pages 34 and 39; D. Fullerton, pages 62 and 63; Illustrated London News, pages 66, 67, 77 and 98; Mansell Collection, pages 35, 54 and 59; Marsh Brothers and Co Ltd, page 52; National Union of Mineworkers, page 66; Peak District Mines Historical Society, page 33; Radio Times Hulton Picture Library, page 61 *above*, 71, 84 and 92; Crown Copyright Science Museum, London, pages 14 and 16; Sheffield City Libraries, pages 5, 6, 7, 8, 10, 46, 48, 69, and 85; Sheffield and Rotherham Constabulary, page 96–97; Tolson Memorial Museum, pages 3 and 21. The maps and diagrams on the following pages are redrawn by kind permission of the authors and publishers: page 12 from A H John, The Walker Family, copyright Business Archives Council; page 83 from Sheffield and its Region, copyright Association for the Advancement of Science 1956. The author is grateful to Dr A.R. Griffin (author of *British Coalmining Industry Retrospect and Prospect*, Moorland 1977) for his advice.

Contents

To the Reader

South Yorkshire is not entirely a region covered with coal mines and iron works for it still has many villages set in pleasant country. Yet if you make the journey from Sheffield to Leeds, either by rail or by the new motorway, you will see all around you collieries and iron and steel works, together with other industries that have grown up with them. You will also be able to see remains of old, derelict works some of which date back to the Middle Ages when monks from the abbeys of Yorkshire were mining and smelting the iron stone.

As you read this book you will discover how the early mine owners and iron masters were connected with agriculture, but as inventions and new ways of making things were introduced, they changed their methods. As the older firms faded away, so new ones took their place and what had been local industries became national ones as the result of improvements in transport. Most important of all you will see how the lives of people were affected by this change in very many ways.

When you have read the book, you may be able to find out how these changes affected the area in which you live, for there are many interesting things still to be found out about industrial changes.

The Yorkshire, Derby, Notts Coalfield showing coal seams

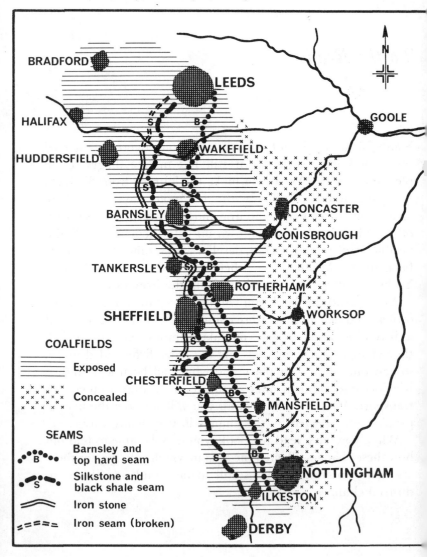

BRADFORD

LEEDS

GOOLE

HALIFAX

HUDDERSFIELD

WAKEFIELD

DONCASTER

BARNSLEY

CONISBROUGH

TANKERSLEY

ROTHERHAM

SHEFFIELD

WORKSOP

COALFIELDS

Exposed

Concealed

CHESTERFIELD

MANSFIELD

SEAMS

Barnsley and
top hard seam

Silkstone and
black shale seam

Iron stone

Iron seam (broken)

NOTTINGHAM

ILKESTON

DERBY

1 The Manufacture of Iron

In South Yorkshire, iron ore was mined from the seam that lay over the top of the Barnsley and Silkstone coal seams. This seam is called the Tankersley seam because the quality is good in the neighbourhood of Tankersley, but the seam itself stretches from Huddersfield to Sheffield. Now if you look at the map of the coalfield you can find out for yourself how the seam of iron stone is in the coal *measures*. The thickness of this seam is $11\frac{1}{2}$ inches and was first mined from *bell pits* or by *adits* from an *outcrop*. The earliest bell pits in South Yorkshire date from the thirteenth century when monks from Byland Abbey were seeking permission to mine iron stone. In the register of Archbishop Gray of York (1215–57) there are references to the mining of iron at Silkstone and Tankersley. The methods of mining iron stone and *smelting* changed little until the eighteenth century.

If you look at the illustration on the next page you will find

Bell pits at Emley, Huddersfield

3

out why they are called bell pits. The pit was sunk to a depth of twenty feet and worked outwards from the bottom of the shaft, as the diagram shows, until either ventilation became too poor or the roof began to fall down. A new pit was then sunk and the old one filled in. If the iron stone was mined by an adit then it would be like the one in the illustration opposite, where the iron and also coal were pulled up a small incline following the seam and allowing the water to drain away naturally.

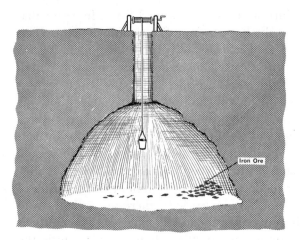

Plan of bell pit

The iron ore was piled up in heaps or stacks and allowed to stand for a few months or even a year until the weather had cleansed the stone. The lumps of stone are called *nodules* and are sometimes as large as a man's fist or as small as a walnut. Two bell pits could produce 500 loads of iron each year. This word *load* may seem a strange one to you but you must remember that the old system of weights was used until the middle of last century. A load is $2\frac{1}{2}$ cwt, so you can work out the total weight of 500 loads. A weight of $6\frac{3}{4}$ tons of iron stone was needed to produce one ton of iron. This $6\frac{3}{4}$ tons was often called a dozen of iron stone.

The stone was then taken to the furnace, which was never more than two miles away from the mine, where it was sorted,

Adit mine, Derbyshire

washed and *calcined*. The charcoal for smelting the stone came from distances up to fifteen miles, or wherever suitable wood was available. In Sussex whole forests were felled for conversion to charcoal and by 1750 there was a shortage of wood, but in South Yorkshire instead of cutting down the forests to produce charcoal, woodland known as 'spring woods' was used, that is woods of oak and ash about fifteen to twenty years old. Sometimes hedge wood was used. The men who burned wood for charcoal were known as *colliers* and a collier was paid sixpence for cutting and *cording* 128 cubic feet of wood for burning. His average wage was one shilling a day. The charcoal was taken to the furnace either in *bannisters* or in *paniers* carried on the backs of ponies. A large furnace could keep six gangs of men employed in cutting and making coal. The illustration on page 6 shows how this process was carried out.

During the century from 1660 to 1760 the Spencer family of Cawthorne whom you met in 'The Agrarian Revolution' had, either by purchase or by marriage into families connected with the iron trade or taking partners like the Cockshutt family, obtained control over all the furnaces which were scattered over an area of forty-five miles.

The furnaces varied in size but they were all similar to the one shown in the illustration. The number of men employed at each furnace was seven: two *founders*, who had the charge of controlling the blast of air from the bellows and tapping the furnace when the iron was liquid; two *fillers* who placed charcoal, iron and limestone in baskets and fed the contents into the furnace; two *riddlers* who sifted the unburned charcoal from the slag to be used again. There was also a man in charge of the bellows, *goits* and dams. In front of the furnace was a bed of sand with a long channel running down the middle and a number of short ones branching off. The liquid iron ran into these channels. Since the early founders were also farmers they gave the name 'sow' to the long channel and that of 'pig' to the shorter ones because this pattern reminded them of a sow feeding her young pigs. When the iron had filled these channels it was allowed to cool and then broken into short lengths for delivery to the forge. A modern furnace, after lighting up, continues to work for seven days each week throughout two or three years, but these early furnaces only ran for twenty-four to thirty-two weeks in winter and where a modern furnace produces 300 tons a day, these produced but two tons of iron. The furnace at Chapeltown, Sheffield, in the winter of 1761, was in blast for twenty-six weeks and four days, producing a total of 352 tons of iron which made a profit for the company of 10s 2½d per ton.

Charcoal burning near Stocksbridge, Sheffield

Furnace with pig beds in Staffordshire

In the summer months when the furnaces were idle repairs to the interior took place and the bellows for providing the blast of air to the furnace were repaired. The Spencer-Cockshutt partners employed William Osborne to look after their furnace bellows. Below you can read the account he sent to Mr Spencer for repairing the bellows at Barnby Furnace, Cawthorne in 1761.

5 sheep skins	5*s* 10*d*	
oyle-tallow	5*s* 10*d*	
5 cow hides 132 lbs at 8*d*		
2 bull hides 100½ lbs at 8½*d*		
2 cwt 3 stone of nails	£6 17*s* 1*d*	
Bellows boards	£10 10*s* 0*d*	
Total Cost	£43 12*s* 2*d*	

'N.B. Bellows boards and some hydes not yett paid for.' A set of finished boards in ash could cost as much as £21 4*s* 8*d*. You can see how expensive it was to repair the bellows and this does not include the repairs to the water wheel and *water courses*.

The pig iron was taken to the forge where it was heated in an open furnace, with charcoal, called a *chafery*, and hammered out in the *finery*. The largest forge was at Wortley and here you can still see the old method of producing iron bars.

Tilt hammer at Wortley forge, Sheffield

The illustration shows you the old *helve* hammer worked by a water wheel to beat the iron into a square bar called a *bloom*. The next illustration shows you the old type of *bloomery* where bar iron was made. This was the method used until Henry Cort designed his *puddling* furnace in 1783. The iron bars were then cut up in a slitting mill into sizes suitable for nailmakers and blacksmiths. The men who worked at the forges were very skilled in their craft and a man had to serve an apprenticeship of seven years before he could be called the 'Master of the Bloom'.

In time the supply of iron stone ran out and the pits moved eastwards. Charcoal became very expensive as cloth *drawers* and *finishers* began to use it in their trades. Experiments were going on at Coalbrookdale under the direction of Abraham Darby to find a replacement for charcoal as a fuel. He succeeded in producing iron by smelting with coke and at a less cost than using charcoal. After 1760 it was cheaper to buy iron smelted with coke than iron smelted with charcoal so the great Spencer-Cockshutt partnership broke up. The Spencers retired to Cawthorne and became country gentry while the Cockshutts took over the forges and reorganised them to deal with new trade.

Early bloomery with primitive bellows

In 1771 John Cockshutt, now owner of Wortley forge, took out a patent 'for making *malleable* iron, directly from the ore in a finery', which meant *refining* pig iron with charcoal and converting it into wrought iron. In 1783 Henry Cort discovered a new way of making wrought iron. The pig iron was heated in an air furnace fed by coal, instead of placing it in the finery. There were holes in the furnace doors through which the workmen could push bars to stir up the iron until all impurities were removed. The clotted lumps of iron were then removed and hammered into slabs before being reheated and rolled. The next illustration shows you the furnace used for producing malleable iron. Notice how very heavy the work seems to be. John Cockshutt heard of this invention in 1787 and went to see for himself. He was so impressed by what he saw that when he came back to Wortley he designed a similar · 9

Puddling furnace, notice the man on the right lifting out a ball of iron

plant for use in his forges and also prepared the drawings for an air furnace for the Cyfarthfa Ironworks in South Wales.

Further changes took place at Wortley in 1796 when the first grooved rolling mill was put in for rolling iron bars instead of hammering them out. This early set of rolls can still be seen at Wortley and is reproduced for you here.

Rolling mill at Wortley forge

2 The Rotherham Ironworks

The villages around Sheffield and Barnsley were centres of the nailmaking industry and at Mapplewell the industry employed about 200 people including women. Here the coal came to the surface in an outcrop and could be used in the nail forge. These forges were like an old fashioned blacksmith's shop, except that there was a special hammer for forging nails, which was worked by a treadle, called an Oliver. The nailmakers had family businesses and an eighteenth-century nailmaster was a man of some standing in his village. It was the custom for nail makers to ride to church on Sundays on the back of a donkey and their brides too always went to church on a donkey, while the labourers and lesser folk walked.

We must now try to find out the way in which a family, the Walker family, changed from nailmaking to large scale manufacture of iron. The map is to help you in following the development of the works. The story begins in 1730 in the little village of Grenoside, some five miles north of Sheffield, where Joseph Walker earned his living as a nailmaker and *cutler*. Joseph and his three sons, Jonathan, Samuel and Aaron like many other families in the district, made common pocket knives, scythes, sickles, files and nails. At the same time they ran a small farm to assist their income from the forge. After the death of Joseph the property was divided amongst his sons. Jonathan took over the farm, Aaron ran the forge and Samuel became master of the *endowed* school at Grenoside where he also manufactured sundials. In 1741 Aaron built a small foundry behind the forge to produce small iron castings, for there were good profits to be made in the metal industries at 11

Map of Walkers Iron Works at Masborough

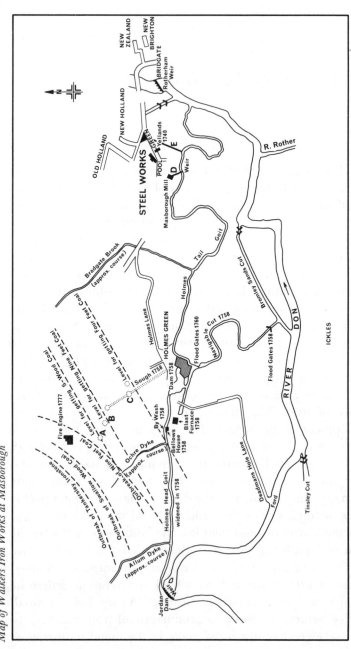

this time and the problems of raising money to finance the business were not difficult. By 1746 the business had grown so much that Samuel wrote in his diary, 'though I thought myself so well settled I began to see the disadvantage of being so far from the *navigable* river'. You must remember that roads were bad and it was easier to use barges on a river like the Don than use road transport. So Samuel and his brothers moved to Masboro', Rotherham, on the banks of the Don, where they built a foundry and forge and also continued to farm. Modern industry tries to place all its production on one site but the Walkers separated their works, building one at Holmes Chapel, another at Conisborough and a third at Thrybergh, all on the river Don to the east and west of the Masboro' foundries.

The first furnace to be built was a charcoal one with the bellows for the blast driven by a water wheel but by 1762 the works had expanded so much that the owners of the water rights on the river brought a *law suit* against the Walker brothers and Samuel wrote this in his diary: 'This year we had great expense in Parliament, and in law, with the proprietors of the River Dun and great expense and loss at the blast furnace.' The reason for this was the large amount of water taken from the river to drive the four water wheels for the furnace and forges. Two years later four new houses were built, with a 'large shop for the frying pan makers: three small shops and an engine or *turning shop* over it'. The firm was expanding and now had a complete staff of clerks, carpenters, smiths, masons and wheelwrights. Their business accounts contain details of the farming, for the clerks were allowed pasture for a cow each. Samuel Walker's diary also tells us about his employees as well as about the business. On 1 December 1774, for instance, he wrote: 'Died. Thos. Whiteley, one of our first and principal clerks: but a sad specimen of the instability of human nature.' Thomas must have behaved badly in some way.

In the meantime another ironfounder, Abraham Darby, the second, had succeeded in smelting iron by using coke in his

13

blast furnaces at Coalbrookdale. By 1750 the new practice of using coke instead of charcoal began to spread. In 1767 the Walker brothers heard of this and built their first coke smelting furnace to produce cast iron more cheaply. At the same time the old forge was extended to include a *tinplate* house. The warehouse too was enlarged and the, 'boring house rebuilt and enlarged at the mill'.

Arthur Young, in his Northern Tour, visited Rotherham in 1768 and wrote this description of the industry he found there:

'Rotherham is famous for its ironworks, of which it contains one very large one, belonging to Mr Walker and one or two smaller. Near the town are two collieries out of which iron ore is dug, as well as coals, to work it with: these collieries and works employ together near 500 hands. The ore is here worked into metal and then into bar iron, and the bars sent into Sheffield to be worked and to all parts of the country: this is one branch of their business. Another is the foundery, in which they run the ore into metal pigs and then cast it into all sorts of boilers, pans, ploughshares etc.'

Newcomen winding engine at Farme Colliery, Rutherglen near Glasgow, built in 1810

Can you state the kind of boilers and pans the company were making and what did Arthur Young have in his mind when he wrote 'etc.'?

The beginning of the War of American Independence led to the Walker brothers expanding their business into the casting of cannon for the army. This meant that extra supplies of water were required, so a 'Fire Engine' was built to pump water. This engine was built to the design of Thomas New-comen (1663–1729) who connected his pump to the engine by a lever beam, to one end of which was connected the pumping gear and to the other the piston which moved in a cylinder into which steam was admitted at intervals. Men called it a fire engine because the power to drive it was generated by a fire under a boiler full of water producing steam. As the war progressed, the demand for guns increased as you can see for yourself from the following figures:

1775	Guns	40 tons 16 cwt
1776	Guns	450 tons 11 cwt
1777	Guns	452 tons 13 cwt
1779	Guns	689 tons 8 cwt
1781	Guns	1220 tons 18 cwt

You will realise that two furnaces would not be able to produce sufficient iron to make all these cannon, so the Walkers had a third furnace built in order to make enough guns for the war. Also more water was needed to drive the machines for boring the guns. In 1776 Samuel wrote in his diary: 'Wall'd a good deal of the goit and built a new bridge over Jordan Dam; a new boring house and improved boring mill greatly.'

Many of you will know how Thomas Newcomen used the steam engine for pumping water from mines and the way in which James Watt improved it. By 1781 James Watt and John Wilkinson had improved the steam engine by adding a fly-wheel so that it rotated instead of merely moving a beam up and down. This meant the engine could be used for blowing blast furnaces, driving forges, rolling mills and textile machines. 15

The illustration shows you how the engine was built, what it looked like and how it worked. We shall have to mention these engines quite often and you must have an idea in your mind of what they were like so that you can understand the changes. Samuel Walker heard of this engine and in 1781 he decided to write to Boulton and Watt at the Soho works, Birmingham, to

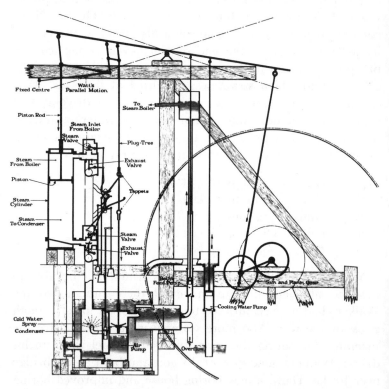

Boulton and Watt's rotative engine 1788.
Drawing showing diagrammatic sectional view

see if an engine could be built to produce the blast for three furnaces. Here is the letter written by Samuel Walker.

'We have some Works upon a River which in general supplies us with Water. In order to make up this defect, in some measure, we are intending to build a Fire Engine, either in the old or common manner or under the Sanction

16

of your Patent. . . . We have coal of our own getting laid down at the Works at about 2¾d cwt and are thinking of a Cylinder 36 or 43 inches diameter and eight foot Stroke and suppose we may work the engine 3 to 6 months in the Year according as the Seasons are wet or dry . . .'

You will have discovered that the engine was to be very powerful and that it was not considered necessary to keep an engine running continuously but only to overcome the effects of a shortage of water if the summer was dry.

On 22 May 1781 a reply was received from Boulton and Watt. They said that they would be pleased to build an engine but they could not sell engines in Yorkshire because: 'The Coal Mines in Yorkshire will not pay us for our attention on that business and we have declined engine orders where Coals are of less value than 4s or 5s a ton . . .' You will understand that the collieries preferred the old expensive type of pumping engine to the new one because coal was cheap.

The Walkers decided to put a new Boulton and Watt engine in the works and Samuel wrote in his diary: 'Pull'd down two shops to make room for a new Fire Engine and rebuilt 'em in the same yard: built and cover'd in a new fire engine house (this a very heavy job).' Of course it would be a big job with all the strong foundation needed for the engine. While all this was going on at Masboro', the mill race was widened at Thrybergh to take a new water wheel to drive the chafery but the great news of the year was in September when Samuel wrote: 'The Fire Engine compleated to blow our three furnaces and began to work this month.'

The Walkers, like so many other ironmasters, were *nonconformists*, so we often find them spending some of their money on improvement to the school or the chapel. In 1781 Samuel built a new school to replace the old one and four years later they, 'erected some new seats about the pulpit; and the Monument to the memory of our good father was put up', in Thrybergh chapel. They also gave a large amount of money to Rotherham Independent College, which was used for training ministers for the Congregational Church.

Extensions and alterations continued to be made every year to the works and when war with France, broke out in 1793, followed by the war against Napoleon, the demand for iron grew very heavy. Walkers now produced 26,000 tons of cannon each year. Between 1802 and 1815 they made a fortune but after the Battle of Waterloo, which ended the war, prices of iron fell because no one wanted cannon and guns. Furthermore the supplies of iron stone round Rotherham were running out so the Walkers decided to leave Rotherham. In 1820 a new company was formed to take over the iron works at Gospel Oak in Staffordshire and to close down the Rotherham works.

You may think that the closing down of the works would mean that the men who were employed there would have to live on parish relief, or the dole, but unlike other employers of the time, the Walkers made sure that those who had served the firm well were not treated as useless persons. Notices were given to the clerks that cows would no longer be pastured on the land belonging to the company and that the clerks themselves would have to find employment somewhere else. A list of the names of clerks who were too old to seek new employment was made and these were given an *annuity*, that is, a fixed income for the remainder of their lives. Then a list of 'old infirm workmen of good character who are to receive pensions' was drawn up. Walkers must have been far ahead of their time for it was very unusual to help workmen in this way during the nineteenth century. They were paying what were, in effect, old age pensions almost a century before the government introduced them.

So the old methods of making iron at Rotherham came to an end, but as we shall see later, men who had learned their trade with Samuel Walker introduced new methods and expanded the Yorkshire iron industry. Before looking at this, we must turn our attention to the coal industry for the two were going to be closely connected in the future.

3 Early Coal Mining

Coal has been mined in South Yorkshire since the Middle Ages. A very early *lease* of a coal mine at Clayton West, Huddersfield dated 1659, gives details of how the mine was to be worked. No more than five men are to be employed at any time, no coal is to be mined in haytime or harvest, for the miners are to help in this work, and finally the landlord is to have his coal 'pit free', or delivered without any charge, for his own house fires. Before you can understand how collieries work, you must first learn how coal is mined.

On page 20 you will see a plan of some colliery workings which shows you the methods of mining. The early method was to drive roadways known as stalls through a coal seam and then remove all the coal over small areas (these are the ones marked A on the diagram), leaving large pillars of coal, rectangular in shape, to support the roof. This is known as stall and pillar mining. At a later stage these were removed as marked at B. When workings were *shallow* this led to subsidence of the surface in uneven ways, so only in very special cases were the pillars of coal removed. The modern method consists of driving a long straight *heading* in the seam and taking out the coal by what is known as 'long wall face'. This method was introduced from Shropshire into Yorkshire after 1840 and is marked with letter C. This method of mining coal is much cheaper for it costs less to support the roof and subsidence of the ground above takes place much more evenly and regularly than by the old method. All this information will enable you to understand the details about mining that you will meet later in the book.

Elsecar Colliery, near Barnsley, is one that has a very long history and we are fortunate that Earl Fitzwilliam's steward

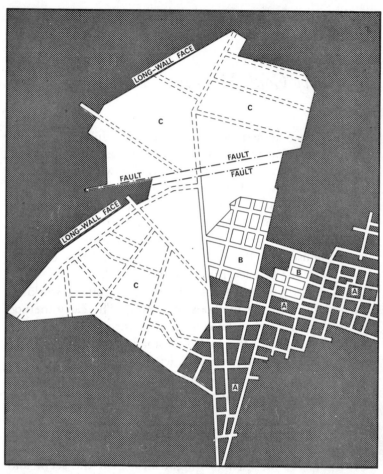

Underground mining plan showing methods of getting coal

preserved the records of the mine. We know that the pit was at work before 1750. In that year Richard Bigley made a contract with the Marquis of Rockingham to mine coal, 'in a certain *close* in Hoyland . . . called Great Arm Royd'. He was not to employ more than two men in getting the coal and he had to make a drainage road so that the water would drain away naturally from the mine into a *sough* or dyke. If it was impossible to get the water away easily then a wooden pump like this made from a hollow tree and worked by a boy, had to be used. This pump was found in old workings at Speedwell Colliery, Emley Moor and is preserved in the Huddersfield museum, at Ravensknowle Park.

Wooden pump at Emley Moor

The first accounts are dated 23 September 1752 and are given so that you can see how much it cost to mine coal. Also you will notice that there is no mention of an engine of any kind.

To the colliers getting 24 pitloads of coal	£2	0s	0d
For filling and barrowing 5 loads each	£1	0s	0d
To two men for drawing 5 loads each	£1	0s	0d
To the horse at trailing to the stack at 2d a load		4s	0d
Joseph Hague—Ten days setting up and keeping accounts		11s	8d
The neat charge	£4	15s	8d

A year later Joseph wrote in his account book: 'No coals pulled at Elsecar Colliery for eight weeks because the pit head overstocked with coal.' So you see that only local trade kept the colliery at work, for the *turnpike* road was some distance away, and when coal stocks piled up the pit had to cease work for a time.

If your father is a miner you will know that he is supplied with coal for use at home on the payment of the cost of delivery. This custom is a very old one, for in a letter from Thomas Smith to the Marquis of Rockingham we read:

24th Feb. 1753. 'May it please your Honrble Lordship. It has been the custom for the colliers & other pit men to have a weekly pull of fire coals paying sixteen pence per Dozen, the price of getting; they humbly desire yor. Lordship wod. comply with the above custom.'

Gin at work

The next step was to install a *gin* or engine worked by a horse to improve the lifting of coal from the mine to the surface. The illustration shows you one of these gins in position and you can see the track round it made by the horse. A long rope was fastened to the drum from the tubs of coal and the horse was harnessed to the cross beam so that as it moved round in a circle it turned the gin and pulled the tubs of coal. You can see this quite clearly in the illustration here. When the gin was working at Elsecar, Thomas Smith wrote to the Marquis of Rockingham about it.

'May it please yor. Honble Lordship.

I have erected a Ginn at the Pit at Elsecar which I hope will answer the End very well and have Employed the two *Naggs* according to yor. Lordship's Order which will do very well in time. The horse pulls well in the Ginn, the mare has not had much practice yet because of the sale. I put them to work on Monday 15 Instant and we have pulled thirteen pit loads this week. So wages of the horse this week is £0–4–4. Wages of the mare is £0–2–2. The charge of pulling will be 5*d* p.load and Trailing to Stacks nought.

This from your Lordship's Most Humble Dutiful & most
obedient Servt.

Thos.Smith.'

You will notice that Thomas Smith uses capital letters any-
where and he is quite pleased with the easy way in which coal

can be drawn from the pit. The expenses of running the gin are given so you can see for yourself how much easier it was than by the old way.

Pd to Jin Boy 12 days at 5*d*	5–0
Letting men down	1–3
Letting 2 horses down	4–0

In 1769 three men were paid 2*s* 8*d* to repair the gin and on 18 November a Mr Bower supplied a 'Quart of oile for the Gine—8*d*'.

For many years barrows were used for transporting coal underground and later tubs or *corves* were used drawn by horses or by child-ren. The corves were prob-ably like the one in the pic-ture. A drawing of Elsecar colliery made by Joshua

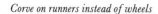

Corve on runners instead of wheels

Biram in 1793 shows a horse drawing a kind of sledge. Coal was taken from the pit top to the coal stack in these corves or sledges, for the ground about the pit head, which was in a field, would be churned up and quite useless for wheeled traffic. Here is an account for repairing these corves in 1769.

Ironing a pair of Corves and mending a shouffel	3–3*d*
A pair of Corves ironing	2–0
8 corf *slipes*, 12 staples, 2 stone nails	12–4
A shuffel mending	7

The slipes mentioned were probably the runners of the sledge. Nails and shovels for the miners came from the local smiths. The coal was taken in baskets from the coal face to the corves, which were later replaced by tubs on wheels.

At Elsecar the steep slope of the ground between the colliery and the Needle Eye monument helped the mine to be ven-tilated naturally but in many cases this had to be done

23

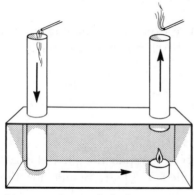

Diagram to show ventilation by upcast shaft

artificially. As the diagram shows air was drawn down the main shaft and through the workings by placing a firepan at the top or bottom of a second or *up-cast* shaft. This you will realise was very dangerous if the pit became filled with gas. At Elsecar a firepan was used, for in August 1769 the pit was full of fire damp and Michael Hague was paid one shilling and three pence for 'fetching the fire pan and Clearing the pit when full of Damp'. The roof of the pit was supported by wooden props or punches which were cut in the local woods. In October 1778 John Wood worked two weeks, 'Felling and Boughing punch wood' for Elsecar colliery. In the same way that the workers at Walker's foundry in Masboro had to help with the farm work, so the surface workers at Elsecar had to carry out jobs connected with farming. Between 7 and 16 June 1769 Robert Beaumont received a shilling a day for mending the road round the colliery. At the same time Robert Watson and Thomas Copley received 3s 6½d for 'ditching 17 roods in the Barley Field Bottom'. If the surface ditches were not kept clean and in good repair when they had been damaged by subsidence, then the water, instead of running away along the channel of the ditch would find its way through the rocks into the shallow mine workings and flood the mine.

Other jobs that were done by men about the colliery were in the fields. We read that Michael Hague was paid for 'Care of the pit hill a day while Joseph measured the Hay Stack in the Park'. Women were also employed, not working down the mine, but as helpers in the fields. 'Sarah Hague and Eliza Hardy for *Feying* 15 acres of meadow land and Pasture at 2½d an acre.'

Thefts of property from the pit took place from time to time.

In September 1777 two *warrants* were obtained from Mr Wilkinson, the local justice of peace to search for 'two Iron Coal Shovels Stolen and several Coal picks'. These do not appear to have been found, for in the following April, William Lockwood supplied four new shovels at a cost of 3s 6d each.

From time to time surveys of the pit were made to record the quantity of coal taken out during the year. This was to enable an estimate to be made for payment of *royalties* to the owner of the land. In October 1779 Michael Hague 'gave John Dickinson men, and Spent *Latchin* is pit 3/6'. (Latchin is a local word meaning surveying.) A letter from a surveyor has been found and is reproduced for you to see how limited was the education of these men. You will see there is no punctuation at all.

'I should have Roate Sooner but Mr Field has been on a jerney and I whanted to see him to know whether he had aney thing in hand with Regard to the Levels for Security of them which he has not after that I Roate to Mr Smith to Meete me at Leeds to Exammon our Plans but he did not attend my Letter has I wished him to write me if he Could not make it Conveniant and I wated upon him and never came.   Yours

       John Harrison.'

The area of coal he estimated as taken out of Wilson's colliery at Kexborough was 7 acres 3 roods 27 perches in 1825.

In 1770 the pit was again idle for there was no sale for the coal and stocks were high. During such times the colliers appear to have turned to farming as the extract from Worsborough parish register shows: '1770 Mary, daughter of William Wood, collier and *husbandman* baptised.' Although coal production varied from year to year the colliery did make a profit.

4 South Yorkshire Coal

The two most important coal seams in the area are the Barnsley and the Silkstone. The former seam outcropped quite close to the town and is more than nine feet thick. The latter lies below the Barnsley seam and is six feet thick. This seam was worked in 1770 by the Old Silkstone Collieries, the price then being 1s 10d for eight pulls or corves (rather more than a ton in weight). But as we have seen the great problem was how to get the coal away from the pit and so this coalfield was not developed until 1850, for transport to move the coal was not easily available before that date.

In 1740 the river Don was made suitable for barges from the Humber to Rotherham, so that Parkgate coal could be sent by water and by 1769 some 300,000 tons each year were being sent to large towns on the river Trent. James Brindley planned a canal from Chesterfield to Gainsborough which was opened in 1773 and so Chesterfield coal could compete with Parkgate coal in the Trent valley. A new canal was proposed in 1777 to enable South Yorkshire coal to meet competition. In the 'Yorkshire Courant' of 11 August 1777 there appeared this notice:

'Whereas it is the opinion that a Navigation from the R. Dunn, near Mexborough, up the River Dearne to Haigh Bridge, near Darton, and a bye branch from the last named place to Barnby Bridge, near Cawthorne, will be of great public utility, a meeting . . . is desired to be held in the House of Mr Francis Roper, the White Bear Inn, Barnsley on 20th day of August by ten in the forenoon.'

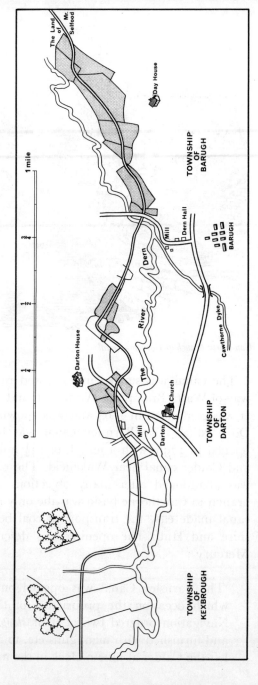

Map of proposed canal to Wakefield 1793. Only the first portion (on the right) was built

Cawthorne branch of Barnsley Canal

The canal was started in 1793 and ran from Swinton by way of Wath, Brampton, Wombwell and Ardsley to Barnsley. It was completed in 1804 and was known as the Dearne and Dove canal. The Barnsley canal was begun in 1793 and opened in 1799, with a length of 14½ miles, joining the Aire and Calder canal near Wakefield. The route through Haigh was abandoned after many objections were received. The branch to Cawthorne basin was the only extension built. The canal made easy the transport of coal between South Yorkshire and Hull. The opening was described in the 'Leeds Mercury':

'The Barnsley Canal was opened on Saturday last. On which occasion the proprietors of the Air and Calder Navigation ordered two of their *sloops* completely rigged and furnished with men, guns etc. to attend. These sloops left the Calder at nine-o-clock in the morning with cargoes of yarn and other merchandise and proceeded to Barnsley amidst a vast *concourse* of spectators, miners and manufacturers who expressed the most lively joy that the opening had taken place. By this Canal, the miner in a rich *mineral* country (hitherto landlocked) and the manufacturers have now the full scope for their varied exertions in the employment of the poor, the farmer in the advancement of agriculture and the whole neighbourhood in the general good of the country at large.'

You will see from this account that the people of Barnsley expected a big expansion in the industries of the town—coal and linen.

There was an extension of the canal to Cawthorne with loading docks at Barugh for coal brought down from Wilson's pit at Kexborough. The illustration shows you the loading dock and warehouse at Cawthorne basin. The little low

Cawthorne Basin warehouse   29

building at the end was an inn called 'The Jolly Sailor', where *bargees* could stay while waiting for coal. A railroad was built from the basin to Silkstone collieries so that coal and iron ore could be sent away by canal. A local barge owner, Thomas Firth of Barugh, carried coal and *sleck* to Goole and brought back limestone, potatoes and apples. Do you know what the limestone was used for? Coal owners made *contracts* with the barge owners and here is one for you to study. You should be able to find out if the barge owner could write:

'I hereby agree with Robert Clarke to work a Keel called the "Robert of Silkstone" in a proper and workmanlike manner as his Captain and Servant. My wages to be regulated by the clear profits gained by each voyage, being after the rate of one third of such amounts. I also agree to take or give one months notice previous to leaving the vessel. his

Signed   George × Darper
mark'

But the canal does not appear to have been very profitable on this section of the route, for in 1807 the directors were complaining that the growth of the collieries had not come up to expectations:

'. . . three collieries are only completed at Barnby, Gawber Hall and Banks. The Barnby Colliery is stopped for the present and at Gawber Hall there is little more coal got than for the supply of Iron Works in the Neighbourhood and these coals are carried not more than one mile on the Canal. The Coals are brought in Carts from Banks colliery to the Canal which is a great drawback as it is a summer Road only. It is usual to see at the Collieries vessels (five to ten in number) which have been waiting for a week to ten days for loading.'

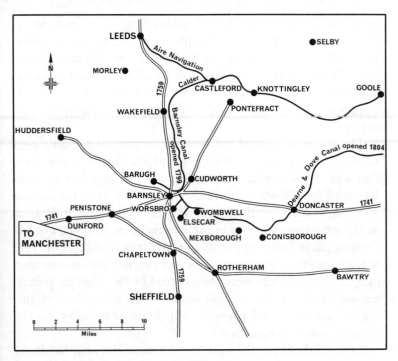

Roads and canals in the Barnsley area to 1869

The solution arrived at was to build a railroad from Barnby to Silkstone but before this was properly completed the railway was extended from Penistone to Barnsley via Silkstone. This meant that the coal could be transported by rail and so the canal declined.

The building of the canal to Barnsley, however, led to the sinking of a new pit at Elsecar. In May 1790, boring began and coal was struck at a depth of 24 to 30 yards. John Hague and Richard Watson received £7 2s od on 24 April 1794 for, 'Boreing for coal near where the Engine Pit is to be at Elsecar in Francis Hardy close at West Corner of Simon Wood'. The seam proved to be good and was nine feet four inches thick. A letter was sent to Earl Fitzwilliam that the coal had been found, 'where the Fire Engine is meant to be fixed in the 31 corner of the close opposite to Michael Hague's house near the Dyke.' If you want to find this place, go to Elsecar gas office. You will then be standing on the site where Michael Hague lived. Fourteen men were paid three shillings a day to sink the shafts and a feast was provided for them when the work was completed. All the stone and timber were brought from local sources.

The working parts of the Newcomen pumping engine were made at Chapeltown, Sheffield and the boiler came from Darwins' of Sheffield. The engine was put together by John Barugh from Chesterfield who was paid £69 2s 0d for the job. The engine *tenter* received 14s a week as wages. The illustration on the next page shows you the engine house and the outside working parts. It began pumping water from the pit at the rate of 1,000 gallons a minute in 1795 and continued to pump until 1923. Electric pumps were then placed in the mine for pumping out the water but in 1928, when the mine was flooded, this engine had to be used again to clear the mine of water, for the electric pumps were stopped.

At the end of 1796 the Low Moor Ironworks, near Bradford, made a steam *whimsey* or winding engine to replace the gin. In 1798 coal was sent by canal to more distant markets than it had been possible to reach before. The increased demand for coal for making into furnace coke for local ironworks led to the sinking of a second shaft, with a whimsey to pull up the coal. Trade was so good that Joshua Biram suggested a new pit should be sunk close to the Milton Ironworks at Elsecar.

You will remember that the period between 1802 and 1815 was one in which England was fighting Napoleon. His attempts to close the ports of Europe to British trade brought unemployment to the Elsecar miners. In order to help the unemployed, for whom there was no dole, Earl Fitzwilliam employed them to build a new carriage drive from Wentworth House to the turnpike road at Hoodhill. When, in October 1812, Napoleon was marching back from Moscow, the ports of Russia and Sweden were opened to British ships once more, so export trade began to revive and in December, furnaces

Elsecar pumping engine, 1795

that had been idle were once more put into blast. This in turn led to such a demand for coal that the collieries were unable to meet it. In order to pull larger quantities of coal, Jonathan Woodhouse from Ashby de la Zouch, a builder of steam whimseys, was ordered to increase the size of the cylinder on the whimsey at Elsecar colliery. In order to meet the demand for coal, a pit was sunk at Rainborough to produce 23,000 tons a year and a second pit was opened at Jump near Barnsley.

In 1833, Joshua Biram who had built up Elsecar colliery died, and was succeeded by his son Benjamin who carried on his father's work. He knew Robert Stephenson, the son of George Stephenson, and together they planned a railway at Greaseborough colliery to move coal from Swallow wood pit to the canal. The full wagons going down pulled up the empty ones. The next illustration shows you the wagons going down to a barge on the canal. At the top you can see the whimsey used for winding coal.

You may by now be thinking that all these improvements and the demand for coal would lead to regular employment. This was not so, for trade, then as now, was never constant, and often there was a struggle to sell coal. In 1832 the only 33

Greasborough Railway, showing whimsey

coal sent to London from South Yorkshire was eleven tons of New Parkgate coal for the use of the East London Gas Company. In the same summer Simpson and Miltas of Peterborough said that coal prices were too high and a London coal merchant, James Shephard said he found it hard to sell Elsecar coal at 16*s* a ton and suggested that it should be given a new name, so Elsecar coal became known as Strafford Main coal. Further trouble came from the ironworks, which owed £17,000 for coal, and there was keen competition from the older coalfield in Durham. Here the Marquis of Londonderry and Lord Durham, who owned a great many large pits, reduced the price of their coal at Newcastle by 4*s* a ton, so that they might cut out Yorkshire coal from the market. The result was that twenty barges of Silkstone coal were unsold at Keadby on Trent.

There was now no other way left but to reduce the number of men employed at the collieries and on 23 March 1833 Ben Biram wrote this letter to Earl Fitzwilliam:

'My Lord,

In my enquiries as to what possible reduction can be made in expenses at the collieries, I find that the number of *hands* could be dismissed and that those who remained could earn better wages at a reduced price by being anabled to get more coals. . . . With this view I have given the men notice of sundry reductions intended to take place at the month's end, and have given notice to leave to 10 Younger men at Elsecar. . . . The number of hands at the collieries have a constant tendency to increase, little boys being engaged at a low wage to attend to the horses, to shut air-doors etc—who as they grow older are appointed to more important posts—and all have the notion that if they behave properly at your Lordships collieries their employment is for life. The collieries by this means become overstocked with men . . .

Your humble servant,
Ben. Biram.'

This was the kind of employment boys were given when entering the mine for the first time. You can see that it would be a very lonely job.

On 20 March Earl Fitzwilliam replied to Ben Biram and as you read the letter I want you to notice that he expresses concern about the way in which the men should be sacked.

Boy opening gallery door

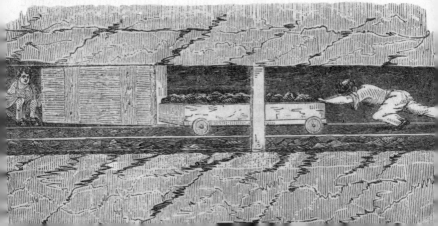

'Dear Ben,

It is painful to dismiss persons in employment but the necessity of *economising* is so great that we must do it, taking care to dismiss those who are of most recent employment. You should also keep your eye on another point viz: that there is no favouritism in the arrangements, for there are a great many relationships which lead to it. The account you give of the *mode* in which the number of grown hands has been increased beyond proper bounds is perfectly natural and should be guarded against in the future . . .'

Poor trade also hit the Barnsley pits, as the following letter from James Porter, the owner of Barnsley Main Colliery shows: 'It appears to me there is a final end and determination of our coastal and foreign trade . . .' He went on to state that they would have to make the best they could of what home trade there was. But in the spring of 1834 there was a slight improvement when Mr Loftus of Hull ordered 24,300 tons of coal for Sweden.

The years between 1825 and 1850 were years when the railways were being extended over all parts of the country, bringing a new and better form of transport to industrial districts. The Midland Railway Company proposed to build a line to run from Derby through Chesterfield, Sheffield, Barnsley and Wakefield to Leeds, but when the route was surveyed it was found that some costly embankments would have to be built and some very deep cuttings made. The map shows you how the line was built over an easier route which bypassed all the large towns except Rotherham. It was the change in the plan that caused Ben Biram to write to Earl Fitzwilliam about the problem that this would cause to coal mines. He said that the only person to benefit from the change would be the Duke of Norfolk, who owned collieries close to the railway. Ben expressed the hope that the Earl would support a railway Bill in Parliament to build a branch line from Rotherham to Sheffield, which would enable other Bills to be put forward for building branch lines from other towns to connect with the main line.

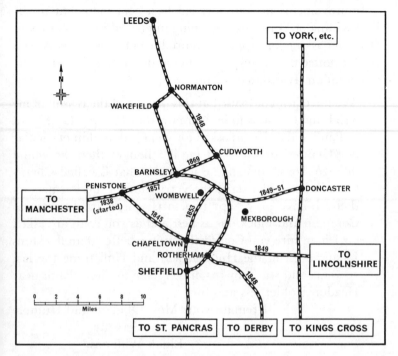

Railways: Barnsley and district to 1869

The problem was solved in 1853 by the building of a railway from Sheffield to Barnsley, running through Wombwell and Elsecar. The nearest point to Barnsley served by the main line was at Cudworth, a village some four miles away, and until 1869 goods and passengers had to be transported by coach to and from Barnsley. There were soon some complaints about the station at Barnsley. Many said that, 'there was no town of equal importance in the kingdom and indeed there are very few villages which have such *execrable* accommodation as we have'. The station had, 'one small room which served as a booking office, for a *spice* stall and the sale of daily papers and as a waiting room'. Another room which was called the ladies' waiting room was so small that a lady of modern dimensions would occupy a considerable portion of it. Ladies who wore *crinolines* took up a great deal of room.

37

Improvements in transport led to a coal merchant in the East Riding of Yorkshire becoming interested in Elsecar coals. His letter asking for supplies is reproduced here for you. As you read it notice the peculiar spellings and that there is very little punctuation. It is dated 6 May 1843.

'We have just got loaded at this place and the reason of me wrighting to you is to let you now that I keep a Coal Yard at Paull and as I ham asked for you Coals and in perticular one Gentleman wo tould me if I bought them he would take 20 Tons from me he leves on what is called Cherry Cobs Sands and I serve the verry most of the Farmers on their. I have only kept two sorts which are Elsecars as Common and Flocktons as best and as you coals are asked for I ham sure you Coals will pay me better than flocktons I have been in the Huddersfield and Hull trade the last 20 years and still remains in it. Please to direct Paull near Headon Holderness and Sir

I remain your Most Obident and Humble
Servent
Elijah Williams.'

Although men like Elijah Williams were prepared to buy coal, yet by 1845 trade was once more poor and some collieries began to give overweight of coal to merchants to attract trade. Ben Birom wrote to Earl Fitzwilliam to say that he hoped the Don Navigation would take over the Barnsley, Dearne and Dove Canals and stop such practices, but trade did not improve, so in 1849 the colliers were almost starving because they had no work. The great change came with the opening of the railway in 1850 and Ben Birom wrote in his diary for 2 February: 'The first train of Great Northern Wagons came up the South Yorkshire Railway to Elsecar this day and were filled each with six tons of soft coals and sent away.'

As a result a man was introduced to Earl Fitzwilliam who was prepared to transport his coal from Elsecar. You may have met him before for he is famous for something other than selling coal. Here is his letter of introduction.

Sharrow Head
24th Aug. 1854

'Dear Lord Fitzwilliam,
The bearer of this note is anxious to be introduced to you to have the opportunity in the subject of conveying coals from this district to the South. I think it best to leave him to express his own views. His name is Plimsoll and you will find him a very intelligent person.

Yours most truly,
Wilson Overend.'

Plimsoll wrote to Earl Fitzwilliam and sent him the poster which is reproduced here for you to see how people advertised

Plimsoll's advertisement

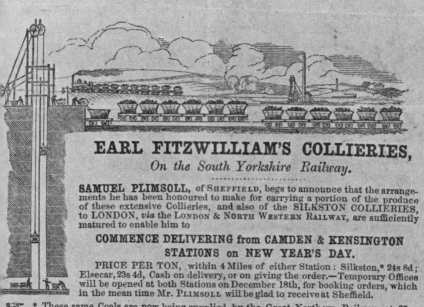

EARL FITZWILLIAM'S COLLIERIES,
On the South Yorkshire Railway.

SAMUEL PLIMSOLL, of SHEFFIELD, begs to announce that the arrangements he has been honoured to make for carrying a portion of the produce of these extensive Collieries, and also of the SILKSTON COLLIERIES, to LONDON, *via* the LONDON & NORTH WESTERN RAILWAY, are sufficiently matured to enable him to

COMMENCE DELIVERING from CAMDEN & KENSINGTON STATIONS on NEW YEAR'S DAY.

PRICE PER TON, within 4 Miles of either Station : Silkston,* 24s 8d ; Elsecar, 23s 4d, Cash on delivery, or on giving the order.—Temporary Offices will be opened at both Stations on December 18th, for booking orders, which in the mean time Mr. PLIMSOLL will be glad to receive at Sheffield.

☞ * These same Coals are now being supplied by the Great Northern Railway, at 27s., his Company having at present, and until December 31st next, a monopoly of the supplies on the South Yorkshire Railway.

in the first half of last century. He said that he was running full trains of 35 wagons of coal on the London and North Western and Midland railways. By Christmas he expected that all the collieries on the South Yorkshire railway would be connected with the Midland line. Unfortunately Plimsoll's hopes were disappointed and he became bankrupt in 1855 as the result of a long railway strike. He then went into another industry. I wonder if you can name this and state what he did there?

Although Plimsoll failed, the improvement in transport led to a big increase in the coal trade, so that when Ben Biram died in 1857 at the age of fifty-five his duties were divided amongst several men, for the mines were now too large for one person to supervise everything. Shafts were sunk to greater depths, reaching 337 yards. The future was bright and by 1870 there were over one hundred pits between Barnsley and Sheffield which provided work for a growing number of people. Many pits were going to produce 1,000 tons of coal a day and a great deal of this was going to be converted into coke to supply blast furnaces as far away as Barrow in Furness.

5 The Milton Ironworks

We have seen how the coal industry changed. Now we must look at the later developments in the iron trade, and see how this led to the great steel firms of Sheffield. Earlier in this book we saw how Walkers of Masborough developed their interests in the manufacture of iron; in 1796 they extended their works by building a furnace at Elsecar where a supply of iron ore was found. Charles Bowns, the agent for Earl Fitzwilliam reported that 'A shaft has been sunk in your Lordship's land between Hangmanstone Tollgate and Tankersley and a very rich bed of black as well as the white mine of ironstone has been found at a depth of 13 yards with a good roof.'

By 1799 a furnace had been built with a Boulton and Watt engine for blowing the furnace, and two fineries for working the iron into bars. In 1811 trade was so good as a result of the demand for guns and war material that a second furnace was built. This furnace was a coke one and the coke was produced at Skiers Hall by a Mr Parker, who also experimented in distilling tar from the coal. The coke was not made in ovens as it is today but by piling coal in long heaps and allowing it to burn away slowly.

The next illustration shows you how coke was made originally. The end of the war in 1815 led to a depression in the iron trade so that in the following year only one furnace remained at work. Trade did not improve, so the Walkers finally closed down the works in 1821 and this led to unemployment in the Hoyland area.

Henry Hartop from Attercliffe works, Sheffield, who took over the Milton ironworks in 1822, had this to say about the

Coke burning at Skiers Hall, Barnsley

conditions in Hoyland when he arrived: 'When first I pur-
chased the works at Hoyland I found there a large portion of
the population in great distress from having been unemployed.
I at once gave those still in the neighbourhood, with some who
left it, regular work and good wages, together with many old
servants of my own. . . .' Hartop, however, was successful in
bringing back some prosperity to the area for he obtained an
order from Isambard Brunel to build two suspension bridges
for the Ile de Bourbon, later named Reunion, in the Mauritius.
Do you know what other things Brunel built besides bridges?
This order led to an increase in the demand for iron ore and
the following letter shows that boring for iron was taking place
in the neighbouring village of Silkstone. George Hinchliffe,
the agent for John Stanhope of Cannon Hall, Cawthorne, who
owned the land, wrote to Mr Stanhope:

'There is a Discovery of a Bed of Iron Stone Breaking out
in Silkstone Fall Wood in that part Now Going down and
which has every appearance of being preferable to any

discovered in any part of your estate. . . . There will be about 50 acres of it and if it prove according to appearance there might be a Foundery Built where Silkstone Mill now stands or by Laying 280 yards of Railroad to Join the original one to the Bason. There is likewise a Bed of fine looking Coal near the Iron ore which I think will prove very valuable.'

George Hinchliffe continued his letter by giving more information upon the state of the woodland and asked his master to return as quickly as possible from London so that something could be decided about the iron.

Joshua Biram also wrote to Earl Fitzwilliam to inform him that the Milton ironworks could take all the coal that three pits could supply and expansion took place at the colliery. In 1823 one bridge was completed and on the 11 November William Newman wrote to inform Earl Fitzwilliam that, 'The Chain Bridge at the Milton Works is the object of universal admiration and it is certainly a beautiful structure and reflects credit on those who made it. . . .' This prosperity did not last for long, for by 1827 trade was once again poor and many were unemployed. The details of the money paid out by the Overseers of the Poor to those who were unemployed and in need of help show you how employment changed from year to year and you will easily find out which were the good years and which were bad.

1822	£630	6s	4d	1826	£271	7s	7d
1823	£510	12s	3d	1828	£393	15s	1d
1825	£279	7s	11d	1829	£645	7s	3d
1831	£576	13s	0½d	1833	£603	7s	1d

The firm of Hartop and Sorby only survived until 1831 when they became bankrupt and sold the ironworks to Graham and Co. who continued the blast furnaces and also made steam engines, pumps, rails and wagons, these items being used on the railways. The company built iron wagons for use on the colliery railway at Greaseborough and also a large steam winding engine which used iron ropes to haul corves of coal up the shaft at Newbiggin colliery, Rawmarsh.

A further improvement in the manufacture of iron was made by James Neilson in 1828. He discovered that if the blast of air blown into the furnace was heated to a high temperature, the amount of coke used to smelt a ton of iron was much less, the cost was less and the production of iron much greater than if the furnace was blown by a cold blast of air. So in 1836 the furnaces at Milton ironworks were blown by the hot blast method and they began to demand more iron ore. They asked permission to get ore from Greaseborough and extend their workings in Tankersley Park. This was given and soon the two furnaces were producing 110 tons of iron each week for the new hot blast system was a success 'and in good fame at Sheffield'. Further mines were opened in Tankersley Park at a cost of £170 an acre. When the mines were exhausted the site was levelled off and restored to its original state. This work of levelling the ground was usually done in the winter to give work to the unemployed.

On 2 March 1838 a famous Manchester engineer paid a visit to the Milton ironworks and later described his experience. Here is part of the account he wrote about it.

'I had occasion to make a business journey to Sheffield and then go forward to York. I had to wait more than two hours in expectation of the arrival of the coach which was to take me to York. The coach had been delayed by a deep fall of snow and was consequently late. When it arrived I found there was only one outside place vacant so I mounted my seat.

'As we approached Barnsley, I observed the blaze of some ironworks near at hand. I was informed that they belonged to Earl Fitzwilliam and were under the management of Mr Hartop. He had given me an invitation to call upon him when next I was in the district.'

He continued by saying that he had met Mr Hartop when he had visited Manchester to buy some *lathes* and other machines.
44 He left the coach and walked across some snow-covered fields

and was made very welcome by Mr Hartop. He stayed the night and was shown over the works next day. I wonder if you have managed to find out the name of this Manchester engineer? It was James Nasmyth the designer of the steam hammer which replaced the old tilt hammer for forging. There was a happy incident as a result of this visit and here James Nasmyth describes it for us: 'The happy chance of my meeting with Mr Hartop's daughter Anne on the 2 March 1838 culminated in our marriage at the village church of Wentworth on 16 June 1840. . . . Fourty two years of married life finds us the same affectionate cronies that we were at the beginning.'

The Tankersley ironstone ran out in time. By 1848 the ironworks had closed and were advertised for sale. As you read the notice of sale on page 46 you will see how large these works were, and you will be able to find out the kinds of machinery and other engineering goods which were produced at Elsecar.

As nearly always happens when a works closes down, many men are thrown out of work. Nowadays they can draw unemployment benefit but in 1848, 75 men and boys at the works and 101 men at the mine became unemployed. The ratepayers at Hoyland met in what is now the Town Hall (at that time the Mechanics Institute) and it was proposed that the churchwardens and overseers of the poor should 'wait upon Earl Fitzwilliam at their earliest convenience stating that the depressed state of trade and the large quantity of men applying for relief or work to the overseers needed help. And request his Lordship's influence with the South Yorkshire Railway or elsewhere to obtain work for them.'

In response to this request, the Earl did succeed in obtaining employment for some of the unemployed on the railway. Others found work at Chapeltown, Sheffield, where Thomas Chambers, a former employee of Walkers, and his brother-in-law Thomas Newton had opened an ironworks in 1793. The war following the French Revolution had caused such a rise in the price of iron that the two partners were forced to find their own supplies of raw material or cease business. Thomas

45

To *IRONMASTERS, and Manufacturers of Steam-Engines, Boilers, Castings, Rails, Bar Iron, &c., &c.*

MILTON IRON WORKS.

TO BE LET, for a term of 21 Years, and may be entered upon the First of October next, all those Old-established Iron-Works, called "THE MILTON IRON-WORKS," situate near to the Elsecar Coal-Field and the Tankersley Park Ironstone Grounds, and at a convenient distance from the Manufacturing Towns of Sheffield, Rotherham, and Barnsley, in the County of York. The Works consist of—

TWO BLAST FURNACES, with every requisite Appendage:—

FORGE and MILL, with Puddling and other Furnaces, Chafery for Drawing Uses, Rolling and Slitting Mills, &c., capable of Manufacturing from 90 to 100 Tons of Finished Iron per Week:—

FOUNDRY, with Pits, Drying Stoves, and every requisite Apparatus for making Engine Work, and Castings of every description, to the extent of 100 Tons per Week:—

ENGINE-FITTING SHOPS, with Lathes, Boring and Planing Machines, Boiler Makers' and Smiths' Shops, and every requisite for carrying on Engine and Railway Work to a large extent:—

Together with an ample supply of ELSECAR COALS, and TANKERSLEY PARK and SWALLOW-WOOD IRON-STONE, on terms to be agreed upon.

The Works possess at present excellent Canal and River Communication, and will shortly have the advantage of the South Yorkshire Railway.

N.B.—Although the Owner of the Works would not absolutely restrain the Lessees from making and Manufacturing Hot Blast Iron, yet he would prefer treating with parties who would undertake to make and manufacture Cold Blast Iron only.

For further Particulars, apply to **Mr. NEWMAN**, of Darley Hall, near Barnsley; or Mr. WOODHOUSE, of Overseal, near Ashby-de-la-Zouch.

Darley Hall, near Barnsley, 15th June, 1848.

Advertisement of sale of Milton Iron Works

Chambers knew that under the estates of Earl Fitzwilliam there were rich *deposits* of iron ore and coal. He approached the Earl who agreed to lease the minerals on his estate to the two partners. The agreement was signed at the Angel Inn, Sheffield on 13 December 1793, and on 1 January 1794 they began to build their works at Chapeltown. By April their first furnace was producing pig iron and production continued until 1942. In 1794 the partners opened an engineering section to meet demands for equipment for ironworks. They were curious about Sir William Murdoch's experiments with gas, which was described as a 'new-fangled and dangerous invention', so they went to Birmingham to see it for themselves. They were so impressed by what they saw that on their return to Chapeltown they began to produce equipment for the making of gas. The expansion in the coal trade led to the building of steam engines by the company. At the time the Milton Ironworks closed in 1848 there was a demand for labour in Chapeltown, the only problem being easy transport to and from Hoyland.

6   Sheffield Steel

Sharpen me well and keep me clean
And I'll cut my way through fat and lean.
I'll wait upon you at the table,
And doe what service I am able.

This rhyme was carved on both sides of Sheffield knives. You will know already that Sheffield is famous for its knives, cutlery and scissors and was so long before the great steel works were built at Brightside. The steel used in the eighteenth

century was made by an old process that was very imperfect. Supplies of iron bars came to Sheffield from the neighbouring forges at Attercliffe and Middlewood. These bars of iron were put into boxes shaped like coffins and between the iron bars were placed layers of charcoal. When these were full, they were made airtight and placed in a *cementation* furnace like the one in the illustration. There they were kept at red heat for ten days to allow the carbon from the charcoal to enter the iron and convert it to *blister steel*.

Cementation furnace, Hoyle Street, Sheffield

Cutler's shop

In 1742 Thomas Bolsover had discovered the art of making Sheffield plate by spraying silver on copper and this had increased the prosperity of the town. Both this trade and the manufacture of cutlery were in the hands of small traders known as 'Little Mesters', for they employed only one or two men. They spent their days working with shirt sleeves rolled up, and in the evenings they sat drinking in the bar parlour of the local inn, discussing local affairs or boasting of British campaigns when the news of Wolfe's success at Quebec or Rodney's victory at the Battle of the Saints reached the town. A 'mester' needed very little money to set up in business; all he wanted was an anvil, a few tools and ready money to buy raw materials. He would either own or rent a shed with a smith's *hearth* in it and employ one or more men and boys. This illustration shows you the interior of a cutler's shop, and you can see some of the processes.

The first great change came with the successful melting of steel in a *crucible* by Benjamin Huntsman. Huntsman was a

49

Casting steel ingots from a crucible

Quaker who had been born at Barton on Humber in 1704 and by 1730 was practising as a clockmaker in Doncaster. He saw the need for better springs in clocks and began to experiment in melting steel in a crucible to produce cast steel. In 1742 he moved to Handsworth, Sheffield, where suitable fireclay was to be found from which he could make crucibles to stand up to the fierce heat. He placed either blister steel or bar iron in a crucible of this kind together with a *flux* and heated it in a coke furnace at a high temperature for four hours. The illustration shows you the furnaceman lifting the white hot crucible from the furnace with a pair of tongs. Before he does this he clothes himself with sacking soaked in water so that his clothes will not catch fire. The steel, which is white hot and gives off a shower of brilliant green sparks, is poured or *teemed* into a mould without splashing. Huntsman's product was not only better but also cheaper than steel produced by the old way.

At first the Sheffield cutlers did not like this new steel, but French firms bought it and in a few years competition from them became so keen that Sheffield cutlers were forced to use it. Some of the 'little mesters' paid Huntsman for the steel in very curious ways. Paul Tyzack paid for his steel in scythes which he produced. Others paid in cloth, corduroy, rum, cheese and other items. Some firms in London seem to have paid by a 'Lottery Ticket' or a 'Half Ticket'. Jedidiah Strutt, who was the partner of Richard Arkwright at Cromford mill, used Huntsman's steel in his machines.

The *slump* in the trade of making files that took place after 1815 led to several cutlers turning over to steel making. The Doncasters had been cutlers for centuries when Daniel Doncaster the second rescued the family fortunes by building a steel furnace in his father's orchard. The same slump brought Charles Cammell from Hull, with £5 in his pocket, to work in Sheffield and later to build his works at Brightside. John Brown and Mark Firth were men who came from cutler families. James Marsh, who had made a fortune out of the Napoleonic Wars by using Huntsman's steel, built a large new works in Pond Street which he divided up in sections for making knives, razors, table knives and tools. By 1835 he had also built a rolling mill and six forges. On page 52 is an advertisement for John Marsh's business. Notice how it is designed and how much it differs from the ones we see today. How many of the products advertised are still in use?

But change was on the way, for in 1836 George Stephenson was building the North Midland Railway line from Derby to Leeds, which was to pass through Rotherham. In 1838 a branch line was opened from Sheffield to Rotherham to connect with the North Midland line and in 1840 there was a through train service between Rotherham, Sheffield and London. The opening of the railroad led to the great *trek* of manufacturers to Brightside which was begun by Spear and 51

MARSHES & SHEPHERD,

PONDS WORKS, SHEFFIELD,

Manufacturers

OF

TABLE KNIVES AND FORKS;

SHOE, BUTCHERS', BREAD & PALETTE KNIVES;

BUTCHERS' AND OTHER STEELS;

FINE RAZORS;

Warranted Cast-Steel Files;

AND

HAND, PIT, CROSS-CUT MILL AND CIRCULAR SAWS.

STEEL CONVERTERS,

AND

MAKERS OF CAST, SHEAR, COACH SPRING, BAR, BLISTER,

AND

GENUINE Ⓛ BLISTER STEEL.

GENERAL HARDWARE MERCHANTS.

ALSO MANUFACTURERS OF

JAMES CAM'S Superior EDGE-TOOLS,

CONSISTING OF

Firmer Chisels, Gouges, Joiners' and Cabinet Mortice Chisels, Socket Chisels, Plane Irons, Drawing Knives, Scotch Screw and Improved Augers, Trowels, Hoes, Mincing Knives, Adzes, Shingling and other Hatchets and Axes, and Coopers' Tools, including the most modern English and American Patterns.

Jackson in 1837 and soon followed by Mark Firth and John Brown. The introduction of Nasmyth's steam hammer in 1849 soon led to firms beginning to open their own forges and do away with the custom of sending steel to forge at Wadsley and Attercliffe.

The coming of the railways and developments in engineering led to a demand for steel castings of larger sizes than had been made before. An ingot of 30 lb weight was the greatest that Huntsman managed to produce. In 1851 an ingot of 25 cwt had been produced for Prince Albert's Great Exhibition by Thomas Turton. But steel was expensive in 1850 at £50 a ton, so experiments were made to try to produce a cheaper steel.

Section showing Bessemer converter

In 1856 Henry Bessemer discovered that by pouring molten pig iron into a converter, which looks like a large butter churn lined with firebrick, and by blowing a strong blast of air through the molten iron the impurities could be burned away, as the diagram shows. The result was steel which was not so high in quality as the old crucible steel but could be used for making rails and ships' plates and was certainly very cheap to produce. The man who made the new Bessemer steel process a success in Sheffield was John Brown.

John Brown was born in 1816. After he left school he was apprenticed to a linen draper but John, who was then fourteen, did not want the drapery trade but a merchant's, for 'a merchant did business with all the world'. His apprenticeship was then changed to a firm of merchants who manufactured files and cutlery. At the end of his apprenticeship he joined the firm of Earl Horton as a partner but soon he decided to branch out on his own. In 1844 he began to produce steel at a works in Orchard Street but he had to move to larger premises in Furnival Street, where he made steel, files and springs for railway coaches. His invention of the conical railway coach buffer in 1848 led to an expansion of his works. In 1854 he   53

The Bessemer steel process at the Cyclops Works, Sheffield

bought a site of three acres in Saville Street and three years later this became the famous Atlas Works, soon to cover twenty-five acres. In 1861 John Brown and Company were willing to adopt Bessemer's process of steel making and to experiment with it. So successful was the result that the works were turning out every four hours some twenty-four tons of cast steel, twenty times the size of Turner's ingot just fourteen years before.

The old forges were too old-fashioned to handle masses of steel of fifteen tons or more in weight. The new forges handled steel as if it were a soft substance. Even today it is wonderful to see armour plate rolled to a correct thickness as if it were dough. Or to see a red hot lump of steel eighteen inches square cut with no more difficulty than one cuts a wedding cake. A lump of metal passed between rollers for a few times comes out in the end as a sixty foot rail perfectly formed. The period after 1860 was one of great expansion in steel.

7 We—the Workers

You have read a great deal about the change in the coal and iron industry and their organisation, but you have not yet heard much about the people who played a part in these changes. All rapid change affects the lives of people and the effects of such changes can often be seen for a very long time afterwards. Many of you will have heard stories about the dreadful conditions under which children worked at this period and think that this was the result of the changes which we call the Industrial Revolution. What also happened was that the new system brought to light the bad conditions of employment under the domestic system. Children had always been employed in domestic industry from the age of five or six, so when industry moved from home to factory all these things became more noticeable. However, as you read this book do not expect to find conditions of employment to be the same everywhere, since you will discover that employment in Sheffield is different from employment in Elsecar. So that you can follow this clearly we are going to look at the life of the miner first of all.

Mining often ran in families and in the eighteenth century it was often combined with farming when trade was bad. The old system of binding a boy apprentice was followed, as this extract from Stainborough colliery shows you. It is dated 1774, and was: 'Between Robert Wyke of Barnsley in the township of Silkstone colyer and William Wyke of the same township as apprentice for seven years'. He had to live with his master who was to, 'Teach, learn and Inform him the said Apprentice . . . in the Occupation of a Colyer which the said Master now useth. . . . And also shall find him the said Apprentice sufficient of food, meat, drink, washing and lodging during the said Term.'

By the terms of the Statute of Artificers 1563 the justices of the peace meeting every year at Easter were to fix the wages to be paid in industry according to the prices of bread and ale. These were the basic diet of working people. Even so, wages varied a great deal from area to area. In the Wakefield district in 1770 wages were from 10s to 12s weekly, and in Rotherham they were from 7s to 9s for working a twelve hour day from 4 a.m. to 4 p.m.

We are fortunate that the details of how miners were paid at Elsecar colliery in 1778 have survived so that you can see for yourself how much they earned. You should with a little care be able to find out which of these were men and which were boys.

Edward Dickenson senr getting 5 loads at 2s 2d	10s	10d
Edward Dickenson jnr getting 4 loads at 2s 2d	8s	8d
Edward Dickenson for driving 10 yards of		
Bordgate at 16d for New Pit	13s	4d
Richard Dickenson for getting 6 loads at 2s 2d	13s	0d
3 colliers allowed for candles and wedges 1s ea.	3s	0d
3 colliers for filling 15 pit loads at 4d	5s	0d
3 colliers Feying Sleck from 10 yards of		
Bordgate at 4d	3s	4d
Robert Watson leading coals 11 days at 1s	11s	0d
Joseph Hague driving the Ginn 11 days at 5d	4s	7d
Richard Watson for stacking coals 5 days at 1s	5s	0d

The conditions of war in 1798 caused the Yorkshire Justices to abandon the custom of fixing wages, for industry was prospering and employers were fixing their own prices. Here is the price list for 1797 which you should compare with that for 1778 to find out how much wages have risen.

Filling 40 corves	2s 6d
Colliers for Levels driving Deep and Counter Levels	2s 6d yd
Cleaning sleck from Levels	4d yd
Thomas Hague leading coals	1s 8d day
William Burtoft stacking coals	1s 0d day
Ginn Driver	6d day
Bordgates driving 3s 6d yd but on account of wet	4s 0d yd
Matthew Stevenson for *Hurrying*	2s 0d day

As is usual in war time, prices continued to rise. The colliers knew that a period of prosperity was beginning and that later the railways would help in this, so naturally they wanted a share. In an attempt to obtain a share of the rewards, the colliers often went on strike. On 21 February 1831 the colliers at Elsecar refused to work and several barges were kept waiting to be laden with coal. The boatmen tried to persuade the colliers to return but they took no notice. They then complained to Joshua Biram who again took no notice of the request of the boatmen, but the colliers thought the matter over and went back to work on the Thursday. In March they were again on strike as a protest against a too stern overman, John Winter. Lord Milton, eldest son of Earl Fitzwilliam, had suspended him but after an interview he was given back his job and this annoyed the colliers, who relied on the support of Earl Fitzwilliam to over-rule too strict officials. The Earl dismissed the man and the colliers returned to work.

In 1836 the colliers were earning from 4s to 4s 6d a day and working a ten-and-a-half-hour day. We are told that John Hunter earned £3, Edward Parker £4 7s 0d, George Hobson £2 5s 6d, Joseph Hirst £3 4s 6d, George Lindley £2 10s 0d and John Winter £2 12s 6d. In April 1836 the colliers were once more on strike, for they objected to screening coal for the ironworks and being paid the price of cleaning slack. Ben Birom suggested that a bonus scheme should be introduced, allowing [to the industrious] an extra price on all coal got 57 above what was considered an average man's week's work, it might perhaps have a good effect'. This sounds a very modern way of payment.

On the whole the miners at Earl Fitzwilliam's collieries were better paid than at most. This is shown in a letter written by Henry Hartop to Earl Fitzwilliam stating that the colliers got 25s to 26s weekly for mining coal by the wagon for a full week. Other mine owners paid only 16s so that 'His Lordship's colliers receive wages 62½ per cent higher than his opponents in the coal trade and so the workmen at Elsecar furnaces are wanting the same'. Not all the miners were so well paid as those at Elsecar as the following letter from the miners of Silkstone to Mr Clarke's agent at the Old Silkstone collieries shows:

'Master and Agent

Dear Sir,
We your humble servants beg leave to inform you that we have drawn up a Statement concerning an advancement of our wages which we present to you hoping that you will accept of it as not being an *exorbitant* one.
Levels Broken at 2/6d a yard. Stright end at 2/4d a yard. Bordgate at 2/0 a yard. Where the Switch and Seat coal is left Wethar Bord or end to be more than above by 2d. Broken end in tops 2/0. Bordgate in tops 1/6d Coals to be 5/10½d a dozen. 13 corves to a dozen or 1/9½ a ton.
And we your humble servants Solicit an Answer in a week from this day April 8th 1844.
                                    From your affectionate Miners.'

You will observe that the letter shows the relations between the miners and the mine owners were still friendly at Silkstone. Their efforts were unsuccessful and after a four months' strike they accepted an offer 4d less than they proposed. The wages of the blacksmith, carpenter and engine tenter were to be 3s a day while pit *datelors* and ginny men were to be paid 2s 4d a day and *hangers on* at 2s 2d.

By this time you should be wanting to find out the conditions under which miners worked. This extract from a poem by Ebenezer Elliot will tell you what he thought. He describes a coach traveller seeing a whimsey at work for the first time.

A Whimsey it is called, wherever seen;
And strangers travelling by the mail may see,
The coal devouring monster as he rides,
And wonder what the uncouth beast may be
That canters, like a horse with wooden sides,
And lifts his food from depths where night presides
With winking taper, o'er the inback'd slave
Who, laid face upward, hews the black stone down.
Poor living corpse; he labours in the grave,
Poor two-legged mole; he mines for half a crown,
From morn to eve—that wolves who sleep on down
And pare our bones may eat their bread—tax warm.

The illustration will explain for you what Elliot is saying in his poem. He also attacks the corn laws that made bread so very expensive to buy for all except the rich people.

Miner hewing coal by hand

It was the custom in very many collieries to employ small children to do the work of opening and shutting the ventilation doors to allow the tubs full of coal to pass through. On p. 61 you see a boy standing beside the door and children are pushing tubs of coal. You will also see that they are using candles for light and this might easily cause an explosion if gas came in contact with the flame. Samuel Hirst of Jump was working as a *trapper* at nine years of age. This is what he said: 'I sit by myself, I never have a light I sit all day long and never do anything except open and shut the door.' George Lindley who worked at Thorpe's colliery at Gawber said: 'I am a trapper at Gawber pit and I have worked three years [he was then nine]. When my light goes out I smoke my pipe. I smoke a *quartern* of tobacco every week.' Girls also worked in the mine and this illustration shows you the girls working alongside the boys, doing the same work and pulling tubs by means of a belt and chain. George Armitage, who had worked in the pits from the age of twelve until he was twenty-two and was now school-master at Hoyland Low school had this to say about the employment of children in mines: 'I hardly know how to *reprobate* the practice sufficiently of girls working in pits. . . . Many a collier spends in drink what he shut up a young child the whole week to earn in a dark corner as a trapper.' Girls were only employed in a minority of districts: in the Fitzwilliam pits there were no girls at all.

Amongst miners, boys were always looked upon as valuable property for they could earn good money in the pits. A widow with a family of boys was much sought after by wouldbe husbands. In one case a widow was stopped by a suitor at her husband's funeral. Her reply to his proposal of marriage was: 'You are too late. I am engaged. I accepted Ben before starting out for the funeral.'

One way in which to prevent miners from moving from one colliery to another was to run a colliery 'Tommy-Shop'. Here the miner could obtain on credit, food, clothes, soap and other goods and pay for them by deductions from his wages each week. This meant that the miner was always owing money to

Children working in the mines

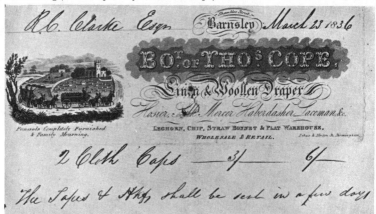

the colliery shop. He was unable to change his employment until the debt was cleared and this was often a difficult thing to do. The bill headings reproduced for you show the kind of things that were bought by the shop. If you examine them closely you will find out some interesting changes in the way people advertise their goods today. This particular shop also sold linen, calico and pottery, this last item coming from Bateson & Co. of Castleford. When a miner was in debt to the colliery shop he had to sign an agreement of which the following is an example.

'As I stand indebted to Mr. R. G. Clarke to the amount of £5 12s od I hereby agree to pay the same by installments say two shillings & sixpence per Fortnight. To commence the first week in August next. Witness my hand this twenty eighth Day of June 1843.

His

Thomas × Haigh

Mark'

If a miner did try to leave his work and go elsewhere then he could be brought back and compelled to work for his old employer until the debt was cleared as the following will show you.

'Be it remembered that Joseph Green, Collier, late of

Bill heading (Paragoric, Epsom salts, Flowers of Sulphur)

Partridge Dale in the Township of Thurgoland having *absconded* the Employment of R. G. Clarke Esqr. and standing at the same time indebted to Mr. Clarke the sum of £2 16s 9½d. for the neglect of his work which amounts to the sum of 13/6d which total sum of Debts and Charges amounts to the sum of £3 10s 3½d. The said Joseph Green agrees to work for Mr. Clarke until the above sum be discharged which is to be stopped out of his wages by 2 Shillings per week as witness my hand this 10th Day of March 1836.'

In addition to the problems of debts and earnings, a miner had to face the dangers of accident, fire, flood, and explosion and some incidents are given so you can understand how dangerous the life of a miner can be. On 13 February 1806 George Boid was hurt by 'a great fall of coals upon him but was thought likely to recover'. He had four children and Earl Fitzwilliam sent one guinea to help him. In December 1808 a fall of roof killed Richard Jessop who left a widow and six children and orders were given that she was to be paid half a crown weekly for life. The next year William Evans of Scholes was injured by a 'fall of coals', and he received 9s weekly as compensation. It was most unusual for miners to receive compensation for accidents but as there were millowners who treated their workpeople well, like Robert Owen, so there

63

were mine owners who believed that their miners should be cared for.

The services of a doctor were rarely supplied by the colliery owners but in 1838 Earl Fitzwilliam paid Dr Erasmus Stone to attend to the health of his miners at Elsecar. The miners had little trust in Dr Stone and subscribed a small sum of money from their wages each week to pay Dr Crowder. When enquiries were made about this it was discovered that in two cases where Dr Stone had ordered a limb to be *amputated* Dr Crowder had carried out a complete cure.

A serious accident took place in June 1848 when a young winding man was killed at Graham's ironstone mine at Tankersley. The inquest on John Guest, aged eighteen, was held at the Cock Inn, Birdwell Common, and it was found that he had been killed by falling into the gearing of the winding engine. A witness who lived about forty yards from the pit said that he heard the signal bell ringing to indicate that some men wanted to come out of the pit. He noticed that there was no reply to the signal, so he went to see what had happened and found the mangled body of Guest in the gearing.

The monument shown opposite marks the grave of twenty-six children between the ages of seven and seventeen who were drowned in Moorside pit on the afternoon of 4 July 1838. A violent thunderstorm broke over the village and so much water fell that it began to run down the incline to the mine, up which forty boys and girls were coming. As they passed through a ventilating door a rush of water was heard coming towards them. Fourteen managed to get into a *cavity* in the wall, but the rest were trapped by the water, driven back against the closed door and drowned. The fourteen who took shelter got out safely. The bodies of the dead were taken to a nearby farmhouse and then brought in carts to be buried in Silkstone churchyard.

Fire was another danger and when in May 1805 Elsecar colliery was threatened by an underground fire Joshua Birom pumped water down the shaft to put out the fire. Another fire

*Silkstone monument, 1838,
and below part of the inscription*

Take ye heed watch and pray for ye
know when the time is.

> Mark XIII Chap. 33 Verse

THIS MONUMENT
was erected to perpetuate the
remembrance of an awful visitation of
the Almighty which took place in this
Parish on the 4th day of July 1838. On
that eventful day the Lord sent forth His
Thunder, Lightning, Hail and Rain,
carrying devastation before them, and by
sudden irruption of Water into the
Coalpits of R. G. Clarke Esq. twenty six
human beings whose names are recorded
here were suddenly Summon'd to appear
before their Maker.

READER REMEMBER!
Every neglected call of God, will appear
against Thee at the Day of Judgment.
Let this Solemn Warning then sink deep
into thy heart and so prepare thee that
the Lord when He cometh may find thee
WATCHING.

Boast not thyself of tomorrow.

> Proverbs XXVII Chap. 1 Verse

The mortal remains are deposited in
the Graves as undernamed

  1st Grave beginning at the North end.
George Birkinshaw Aged 10 Years
Joseph Birkinshaw Aged 7 Years } Brothers
Isaac Wright Aged 12 Years
Abraham Wright Aged 8 Years } Brothers
  2nd Grave
James Clarkson Aged 16 Years.
Francis Hoyland Aged 13 Years.
William Atick Aged 12 Years.
Samuel Horne Aged 10 Years.

The mortal remains of the Females are
deposited in the Graves at the feet of the
Males as undernamed.

  1st Grave beginning at the South end.
Catharine Garnett Aged 11 Years.
Hannah Webster Aged 13 Years.
Elizabeth Carr Aged 13 Years.
Ann Moss Aged 9 Years.
  2nd Grave
Elizabeth Hollings Aged 15 Years.
Ellen Parker Aged 15 Years.
Hannah Taylor Aged 17 Years.

in 1808 was put out by the colliers with, 'no damage except two ponies with a cough from the smoke'.

The invention of the Safety Lamp was of great value to miners. Sir Humphrey Davy, the scientist designed his lamp by surrounding the naked flame with a wire gauze. If any gas came into contact with the gauze it would put out the light, by cutting off the supply of oxygen, and so prevent an explosion. This lamp and one designed by George Stephenson led to a reduction in the number of explosions in mines, but

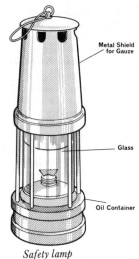

Safety lamp

at first there were rather more because miners took greater risks with the lamp than the candle. Joshua Birom bought one for use at Elsecar colliery and gradually they replaced the dangerous naked light. The tremendous force of an explosion can be seen by examining the illustration of the one that took place at Lundhill colliery, Wombwell in 1857 when the flames shot up the 220 yard shaft and a further 20 yards into the air.

The explosion at Lundhill colliery near Barnsley

The explosion at Oaks colliery, 1866

One of the worst disasters in the history of mining took place at the Oaks Colliery, Barnsley on 12 December 1866. As you can see from the illustration this was a large colliery employing a large number of miners. On that Wednesday morning some 340 men and boys went down the pit and only six of them lived until the New Year. There were forty horses in the pit all of whom were killed with the boy drivers at their side. The explosion took place in the early afternoon when only fifty minutes of the day's work remained. Suddenly there was a terrific explosion and the force of the blast blew the cage up number one shaft (there were three shafts) into the headgear and broke the coupling as you can see for yourself. The broken cage was removed and a new one put on so that a party of *deputies* could go down. At the bottom they found many men all badly burned; the living were wrapped in cotton wool and the dead taken to their homes.

The rescuers worked all the afternoon to try to save the 300 men; at midnight they left the pit to get some rest, for they intended to finish the work next day. On the Thursday morning twenty-seven rescuers were at work down the mine when Mr Minto, the underviewer, walked over to inspect the upcast or furnace shaft. He leaned over the edge to find out the condition of the air coming from the pit. He did so a second time and an explosion took place which rushed up all three shafts at once and knocked Mr Minto down. This meant that the rescuers were all killed. Before ten o'clock a third explosion had taken place when smoke, flames and sparks shot from all three shafts.

On Friday morning, very early, those at the pit mouth heard the signal bell ringing at the bottom of the shaft. Listening carefully they heard a voice, and a bottle of brandy and water was lowered down on a piece of wire. The problem was to reach the man for all the winding gear and cages were destroyed. Close by was a small engine used for sawing wood and this had a drum fixed to it which could be used for winding a rope. A rope was brought, wound on the drum and a very large pan or kettle fastened to a hook at the end of the rope. The colliery manager, Mr Mammatt, asked for volunteers to go down. A youth by the name of Embleton volunteered but the engineer said he must first get permission from his father. The boy's father said, 'Yes, he must go down.' When the engine man said he was too nervous to lower Mr Woodhouse, the consultant mining engineer, and the boy down the shaft, the boy's father stood by the engine man and gave him encouragement all the time.

The two men went down, with the kettle spinning round like a top, for the rope was uneven. The water from the burst pipes soaked them to the skin as it fell with a deafening roar down the shaft. After fifteen minutes they reached the bottom and found Samuel Brown, sitting on a heap of rubbish a few feet away. He said that he was the only survivor. As the two men placed the man in the kettle, they saw the tubs of coal in the distance on fire, raging like a furnace. Eventually all

68

Oaks funeral card

three were drawn safely to the top.

Rescue work went on for many weeks and a year later 260 bodies were still in the pit. Four years later bodies were still being brought up, but for more than 100 men the Oaks Colliery is their grave. The dead who were brought up were buried in Ardsley church yard and this funeral card was printed. The families of the dead could not afford to buy wreaths of flowers so the traditional holly wreaths were used. Today the monument reminds all who see it of the price paid for coal in 1866.

As far back as the 1790s the miners had tried to improve their conditions of work by forming a trade union. Unfortunately the French Revolution had broken out in 1789 and by 1791 the government were afraid that it might spread to England. The members of Parliament had no wish to see themselves taken to the guillotine or hanged from lamp posts so they took action to prevent this happening. In 1799 the *Combination* Acts were passed to prevent workmen combining together for obtaining better conditions or improved wages.

In 1799 there were combinations of workmen formed at Old Town colliery, Barnsley, and at Elsecar. Ben Biram gave some information on the reason for the Miners' action at Barnsley. As you will notice when you read it the cause was a reduction in wages at a time when the prices of goods were rising due to the war.

> 'I saw Mr Thorpe yesterday who tells me that every man at his Colliery has deserted by Combination, that he had no agreement with them as to warning or otherwise, the reason for quitting was that he wanted to reduce their price to the same terms as those given at the adjoining and neighbouring Collieries which they would not agree to therefore formed the Confederacy to leave.'

Largely due to the work of Francis Place and Joseph Hume the Combination Acts were repealed in 1824 and in the following year workmen were allowed to enter into peaceful bargaining about hours and wages only.

Though Earl Fitzwilliam's colliers were better treated than those at neighbouring collieries, many miners joined the Miners' Association which was formed at Wakefield in November 1843. At Elsecar the conditions were far in advance of the time for the miners earned good wages, and Earl Fitzwilliam provided his men with good comfortable houses designed by John Carr, the York architect. He wrote: 'I have sent my Lord six different kinds of cottages for the Elsecar Colliers.' Other things Earl Fitzwilliam provided were medical treatment for miners when they were ill, help to men and their families through payment of money when accidents happened. Free, or almost free, education was to be found at Wentworth, Hoyland and Elsecar, so you can see that in many ways the Earl was providing many of the benefits of the Welfare State, on a small scale, more than a century ago.

But the miners, like the cutlers and steel men in Sheffield, had heard of the changes brought about by the Reform Bill (1832), the Poor Law Reform Act (1834), the Chartist Movement (1840), and the Report on Working Conditions in Mines (1842), and they wanted to have a share in the changes and to move with the times. Ben Biram attended a meeting of coal owners in February 1844 when Mr Cooper of Worsborough collieries said that they had given notice to five or six men who were ringleaders in the Association. On the following Monday every miner who worked in the Silkstone seam gave one month's notice that he would end his employment. A

Trade union cartoon (popular idea of trades union meetings, 1834)

meeting of miners was held at Hood Hill when about 3,000 attended, along with several brass bands, for Yorkshire miners love a brass band. The speakers encouraged the men not to earn more than half-a-crown a day. By doing this they would soon reduce the stocks of coal and then the mine owners would be forced to give them what they asked for. Ben's advice was, 'to resist to the uttermost any demand coming from that quarter and to discharge any man known to be a member of the Union or a contributor to its support'.

Posters calling a meeting were put up at local collieries and Ben Biram managed to get hold of one which he sent to Earl Fitzwilliam.

'I enclose the handbill for calling the meeting on Tuesday last. I have received it from Mr Chambers of Thorncliffe who writes that their bottom steward, George Shaw, attended the meeting and attempted to reason with some of them as to the impropriety of their conduct but he was soon stopped by the degrading *epithets* and show of fight *evinced* by those to whom he addressed himself. James Uttley, who has just left me, says he was with him at the time and believes he would have been struck but for the protection of some of his relatives who chanced to be near.

'James Uttley informs me that he had reason to believe that several of the men at Elsecar colliery are contributors to the Union of whom John Winter is chief, but he has not positive proof of it. He also feels that Mr Uizard's men are restricting themselves to eight hours a day. Dixon's pamphlet appears to be a statement of local grievances of which there has been but too just a reason to complain.'

On 5 March 1844 Ben reported that the men at Elsecar said that they had no connection with the Association and were anxious not to support it in any way, but as some did remain members the pits were closed down for a time. By 17 April they had been locked out, as we call it, for four weeks, and Ben asked Earl Fitzwilliam to show some sympathy with the miners at this stage.

'I am persuaded that this stoppage has given most of them a proper view of their situation and of the benefits they would be likely to receive from the Union and that another week of play would be an injury to many of them, which they would feel for a long time. There are some I am sorry to hear who would stick out and abuse those who have shown a desire to work; these it would be well to pick out and discharge; and I think it might be well to require every man before he is again employed to sign a declaration that he is not a member of a miners' union and that as long as he is employed by your Lordship he will not become a member of any such union . . . but discountenance them by every means in his power.'

On 20 April 1844 the colliery owners met at Wakefield and at their meeting they agreed not to employ any collier who was a member of a trade union. All miners who refused to work regular hours or to send out of the mine the usual quantity of coal according to the custom of the colliery at which they were employed would be looked upon as though they were members of a union and sacked. Elsecar colliers signed the agreement and said they were not members of the Miners' Association, on condition that if the price of coal was increased then they should get the same benefits as all those miners at neighbouring collieries. A letter from Mr Brown to Mr Clarke shows what the Silkstone colliers did about this matter.

'I have yours and enclose the form of agreement with our Pitmen. All our Worsborough Park Colliers that we can imploy have signed them & given up their Cards and repudiated any future connexion with any Union. About 20 or upwards and the same at Silkstone Main Colliery and begin work tomorrow morning.'

So if you look for any information about the trade union movement in Yorkshire amongst the miners after June 1845, you will find very little until the 1870s. This action of the mine owners put an end to union activities for twenty-five years.

The cutlery trade in Sheffield was organised very differently from that of the coal mines. By 1760 it included also files, razors, scissors and edge tools. The trade centred round the 'little mesters' who employed either a journeyman or one or two apprentices. The workshop was a small one attached to the house, about seven yards by four yards and seven feet high. There was a door in the middle, an anvil, a smith's forge, a fireplace and a grinding wheel at each end. The floor of the smithy was of earth and there were shutters instead of glass windows. Around the walls would be fastened ballads, dying speeches of criminals, accounts of wilful murders and lists of race horses. Sometimes hens, rabbits and other livestock shared the workshop. The quantity of cutlery produced at such a works depended on the size of the waterwheel and the amount of water available to drive it. The cutler had to carry his goods for long distances to sell them, so distribution was slow.

A boy who wanted to become a cutler was bound apprentice by an indenture. He received a small sum of money each week and was fed and clothed by his master. Amongst other things he had to agree that

> 'Taverns and alehouses he shall not frequent; at dice, cards or any unlawful game or games he shall not play, nor absent himself from his master's service by day or night without the consent and lieve of his master; nor do assent unto anything whereby his said master may be damnified. But in all things as a good and faithful apprentice and servant, shall gently and dutifully demean and behave himself during the said term.'

Before a boy became an apprentice he 'went a liking' to his proposed master, and if this led to satisfaction on both sides he was taken to the Cutlers' Hall where he paid a fee of half-a-crown and so became an official apprentice until he was twenty-one. When he was twenty-one he had to take out his mark and freedom by presenting a piece of work before he could begin work as a journeyman cutler.

The 'mester's' wife was always neat, 'well corseted and plump in tight fitting cotton gown, quilted petticoat and shining buckle shoes'. Her husband was 'right Sheffield' in the way he spoke and worked alongside his apprentices. The house was very rarely quiet for the forge hissed and hammered all day and the spinning wheel clattered at night until the master and his wife sat down to supper and to smoke their pipes before going to bed.

The apprentice wore a pair of leather or *fustian* breeches for working, the crown of an old hat or a paper cap, with his shirt sleeves rolled up and a pair of old stocking legs on his arms so that they were protected against the sparks. James Willis describes the Sunday dress of the apprentice.

> 'The church going clothes of our Hallamshire lads,
> Coats twenty years old and their hair put in pads,
> With strong buckskin breeches and waistcoats of shag
> No wonder they put so much money i'th' bag.
> Striped pudding poke nightcaps, worn all the week long
> With broad buckles at shoes both easy and strong.

If you look in a book of eighteenth-century costume you will be able to find for yourself what these garments looked like. To us, their meals would be very dreary, having the same things every day. For breakfast they had a quarter of oats or porridge with a little milk. For dinner there would be broth and meat from stewed fat mutton or cheap cuts of beef. Oatcake was eaten at four o'clock at what was known as 'drinking' time, while supper was the same diet as breakfast. It was thought to be extravagant to eat oatcake that was less than a week old.

The trade of the grinder was not a comfortable or easy one. The dust from the grinding wheels got into the lungs of the grinder and caused *asthma*. Sometimes a grinding wheel would burst while travelling round at speed and kill the grinder. In a dry summer there was a shortage of water so the water wheel or 'dairy maid' could not work or on occasions it broke down. You will not be surprised that they sang this mournful song.

> In summer time we can't work till water does appear,
> And if this does not happen, the season is severe:
> Then our fingers are numb'd by winter frost or snow
> And few can brave such hardships as we poor grinders do.

> When war is proclaimed our masters quickly cry,
> 'Orders countermanded, our goods we all lay by:
> Our prices we must *sattle*, and you'll be stinted too—'
> There's few suffer such hardships as we poor grinders do.

There seldom comes a day but our dairy maid goes wrong
And if that does not happen, perhaps we break a stone
Which may wound us for life, or give us our final blow—
For there's few that have such hardships as we poor
    grinders do.

The grinders were not a savage lot, but were hard workers in their small water-driven cutlery shops in the Rievlin valley as this illustration shows you. When trade was good very few began work before Tuesday, and some not until Wednesday. In the following extract from a poem about this custom, a wife has given her husband a good telling off for wasting his time in the ale house. Her husband sings this verse after she has left.

Now once more in joys be thinking,
Since hard scoldings tired my wife
The course is clear, let's have some drink in
To toast a jovial cutlers life.
Shall we our pleasures thus give o'er.
No! we will good Saint Monday honour,
When brawling wives shall be no more.

And so they continued to drink through the whole of Monday.
    The developments in the manufacture of Sheffield Plate and the results of the work of Benjamin Hunstman led to a demand for steel which in turn meant more people to work in Sheffield, so the number of people living in the town rose from 9,676 in 1736 to 31,314 in 1801. This lead to a big change in the relations between employers and their workmen, for a few men were growing very wealthy from their sales of plate and cutlery and began to expand their business, so more labour was needed. But the numbers of skilled men were too small to meet the demand so that skilled men were brought in from other towns and even travelling tinkers were employed. Here
76   is the description given of them by Samuel Roberts.

Old-style grinding works in Endcliffe Wood (Rievlin Mill)

'They were indifferent characters—many of them bad ones: therefore during the first forty years the journeymen platers were the most unsteady, depraved and idle in the town. The masters could not do without them, nor obtain better. They were forced to give them high wages and to wink at their irregularities. The masters entice workmen from each other by giving them money and letting them get into debt as a kind of security. There were continual disputes between masters and workmen and masters and masters about them.'

When conditions are like this the workmen make a bad use of their power to tell the employers when they intend to work. Again Samuel Roberts said, 'it was no uncommon thing for men in a shop to demand £50 or £100 to support them while they went "on spree" or "on the booze".' In one case seven men who had been absent from their work for a week (on wages advanced by their employers) sent two of their number to ask for another £10 each. They promised to return to work the next week and so the money was handed over. No wonder these men sang this song as they sat drinking in the alehouse.

Lord send us weeks of Sundays,
A saints day every day;
Shirts gratis, ditto breeches,
No work and double pay.

But the employers were rapidly becoming involved in competition for trade and risking their money, so the workers became more and more at the mercy of the fortunes of their employers. If prices for goods increased then wages rose, but if trade was bad wages dropped and finally men were out of work. So the big men controlled the Cutlers' Company and the small men had to work for the large firms or go out of business.

Just as in the coal trade when colliery owners joined together to have more money, or capital as we say, with which to work, so the workers combined together to form unions and sick clubs. You already know that such combinations were for some time illegal and there were many strikes. By 1796 there was hatred between the workman and his employer especially when an employer played such a trick as James Watkinson who attempted to count thirteen to the dozen as bakers did loaves of bread. Here is a verse from a poem written by James Mather to be sung in public:

That monster oppression, behold how he stalks
Keeps picking the bones of the poor as he walks
Theres not a mechanic throughout this whole land
But what more or less feels the weight of his hand:
That offspring of tyranny, baseness and pride,
Our rights hath invaded and almost destroyed
May that man be banished who villainy screens;
78 Or sides with big W — — — — — — n with his thirteens.

And may the odd knife his great carcase dissect
Lay open his vitals for men to inspect
A heart full as black as the infernal gulph
In that greedy, bloodsucking, bone scraping wolf.

You can imagine the workers singing this in the pubs on the feast of 'good Saint Monday' and beating out the rhythm with their beer mugs on the tables. Indeed it was sung for many years long after the reason had been forgotten.

In 1792 the attitude of workmen in Sheffield was beginning to worry the government, who sent Colonel de Lancey to report on what he found. He said that there were few persons with sufficient influence to resist them in case of riot. He went on to state that, 'as the wages given to the journeymen are very high, it is pretty generally the practice for them to work for three days in which they can earn sufficient to enable them to drink and riot for the rest of the week, consequently no place can be more fit for seditious purposes'. In fact the only authority in the town were two justices of the peace who came once a fortnight to deal with any cases that arose. 'One of these lives fourteen miles away and the other, since the mob burned part of his property, comes very seldom to Sheffield'. He gave an example of how the colliers of the Duke of Norfolk got an increase in wages. 'They refused to work unless their wages were raised, in consequence of which application was made to a magistrate to interfere but he would not, saying he must leave the country. The master cutler also refused so their wages have been raised which must increase the price of coals and also the manufactures of the town.'

In 1810 Thomas Sutton wrote to Stuart Corbett, J.P., that trade in Sheffield was in a bad state and he feared a riot. He said that the men were all combining together to obtain an increase in wages and the masters were combining against them. 'How the contest will terminate I think it would be difficult to say. In a riot most probably. They are writing upon the walls: "Cutlers stand true". Their plans are well organised.' 79

By 1814 this had again changed. Now there was a demand for men to work in the cutlery shops and tool works, so the workmen combined together to demand bigger wages and if these were refused a strike was called. John Spencer writing to Viscount Sidmouth about the trouble on 14 March 1814 said:

'In Sheffield where I was . . . I find that three bodies of workmen had struck and their employers have complied with the terms they demanded; the file makers have demanded an increase of wages and have sent out to the masters the terms they will work for in the future. These file makers get in six short days 25s to 35s and are demanding 15 per cent above that price. Other workmen are doing the same and also the same at Nottingham.'

A year later in the early part of September, a master cutler, Joseph Raworth, wrote to Earl Bathurst about the state of combinations of men in Sheffield. He had bought his business from John Humphrey and unless some action was taken he would be ruined. Here is the letter for you to read. Raworth, you will find, thinks that the law is too 'soft' with offenders and should be more severe.

'I hope you will excuse the liberty I have taken in wrighting you but as a loyal subject I think it my duty to inform you the state of combination in Sheffd. About 6 weeks ago my brother and myself thought it prudent to discharge one of our men for combining with the rest to compell us to give a price that they think wright, and not doing one months notice as the custom of the town but whent, it was only two weeks gon that he was ordered by the committee to strike on the Monday. This we did not know until the Wednesday but on the Tuesday we sent him a note saying if he did not com to his work we should put a nother man in his place he being borer of the scissors. We got a man in his place but he soon informed us he dare not continue any longer as the other had struck work by order of the committee and said there would be a meeting of the workmen in the trade at the Rose and Crown Inn. . . .

'The law is ineffective for the utmost punishment is

three months imprison-ment and they would send them in coach and four there and the same back again and support their familys and would fulley stop you from making anything more, so if we was to do that it would be the ruin of our business.'

The man dared not continue to work for he was afraid that if he did so, the workmen would 'ratten' him, that is break his tools or if he was a grinder damage his wheel so that he could not work. Those who worked for less than the committee stated were punished.

The trades in Sheffield, like the coal trade, went through periods of good times and bad between 1815 and 1850 but the really disastrous year was 1842 when unemployment was very high. The practices of 'rattening' grew in this period and extended to the steel workers as well as the cutlery makers. In 1859 James Linley was killed by a shotgun and in 1861 gunpowder was exploded in the house of George Wastnidge where a woman lodger was so badly burned that she died. Even Mark Firth, the steel maker, received a threatening letter.

'Gentlemen: the game works merrily and we brush away all obstacles before us. If we appear to be rather long about it you see we are none the less sure. It is your turn next and the man who pays back would be the first to get it. If I but move my finger you are sent to eternity as sure as fate. Be advised and take the hint in time.

Mary Ann.'

The settlement of these problems is outside our study in this book for it was all part of the long struggle for better wages and better conditions of work. It is now time that we took a look at the way in which towns grew as the result of changes in industry and discover the conditions under which people lived who came to work in Sheffield and district.

8 The New Towns

If you look at this illustration of Sheffield, made about 1760, you will see that it looks little more than a 'large village in amongst villages'. The buildings are thickest on the hilly area to the west and south, with a small area of buildings clustered close together round the Market Place and Snig Hill. These streets in the centre were very narrow and in Trippet Lane two carts could not pass while the houses jutted out so far in Church Lane that

Sheffield c. 1760

> With roofs nearly meeting, a dark dreary street,
> Might justly be styled the robbers' retreat,

while the side lanes were only tiny alleys. Samuel Gosling who was living in Sheffield when our story begins tells us that the streets were paved with *grindle cowks*, sloping towards a drain in the middle filled with all kinds of filth. At night the oil lamps in the streets were often out and a tallow candle in a shop window did not help. Inside the church there was as much gloom and damp as outside in the streets.

Before advantage could be taken of Thomas Bolsover's invention of Sheffield Plate and Benjamin Huntsman's discovery of cast steel it was necessary to have good roads. When Arthur Young travelled between Sheffield and Rotherham in 1769 he wrote, 'the road is execrably bad, very stony and excessively full of holes'. They were little better than cart tracks. However, between 1739 and 1818 no fewer than nineteen turnpike roads were built from Sheffield to other parts of

The growth of communications round Sheffield

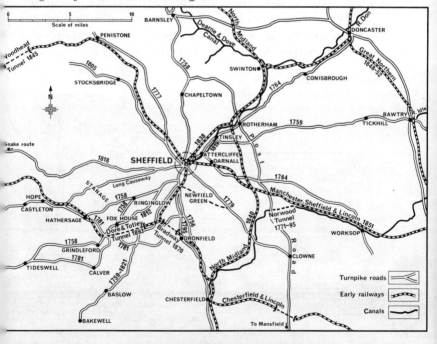

the West Riding, Lancashire and Derbyshire. The diagram shows you where the roads were built and the direction in which they ran. There was transport by the river Don to Doncaster from Bawtry, some twenty miles away, but not until 1819 did the town see boats sailing from Tinsley direct to the sea. The stage coach began to connect Sheffield with the outside world in 1738 and a century later no fewer than thirteen coaches left the Tontine Inn daily.

If you look at the illustration of Sheffield from Attercliffe in 1819 you will see that industry is creeping forward and smoke hangs over the surrounding countryside as the population increases from the 12,000 of 1750 to the 55,000 of 1820. Sheffield became interested in railways to cope with the increasing trade. In March 1831 support was given to a petition to build a line from Manchester to Sheffield.

> 'A large proportion of the advantages of the manufactures of Sheffield is consumed in Manchester or exported from Liverpool, and there is no other way of transporting this merchandise than by horse and cart over the mountains of Derbyshire . . . or by a route of ninety miles through the Yorkshire canals, which is expensive. It now requires two days to go from Sheffield to Manchester and back but by a

Sheffield from Attercliffe, 1819

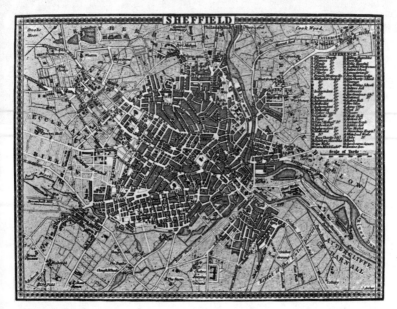

Sheffield in 1830

railway it can be done in one day with six or eight hours
for transacting business.'

This plan was not fulfilled until 1851 and until then the only
railway was the North Midland from Rotherham to London
with a branch line to Sheffield and even this had been opposed
by the people of Rotherham who did not want the 'idle,
drunken, dissolute portion of Sheffield community to flock to
Rotherham.'

The map of Sheffield for 1830 shows you that the town had
grown and changed entirely from that of 1760, for by this date
there were 100,000 people, almost half of whom had come from
the countryside around to live and work in Sheffield. This
meant that houses had to be built very quickly for these people
to live in, and the easiest way to do this was to build back to
back houses in Heely, Crookes and Owlerton. The houses
were built of brick with slate roofs. They had cellars, living
room, bedroom and attic. The living room was used as a   85

Aerial view of working class houses in Leeds

kitchen, scullery, dining room, washroom, bathroom, clothes drying room, with a coal fire and side boiler for heating water. The parents and young children shared the bedroom and the older children the attic. The houses were joined together by narrow, badly paved, undrained and filthy courts. The only time that the streets were cleansed was when Barker Pool was allowed to run into the neighbouring streets. Samuel Roberts describes this event for us: 'Some people were throwing the water up against their houses and windows; some raking garbage into the channel; some washing their pigs; some sweeping the pavement; young children throwing water on their companions, or pushing them into the widespread torrent.' This cleansing took place about once every three months.

At the same time as the cheap, shoddy working-class houses were being built, residential estates were being laid out in Broom Hill, Park Hill and round Sharrow. We are fortunate to have a survey of housing in Sheffield drawn up by two men Haywood and Lee. Here are a few extracts to show you how bad some of this was.

'Bridgehouses. The streets in this area are unpaved but water stagnates into filthy pools and children smear their clothes with this and carry it into houses which make these filthy.

From Iron Bridge to Saville Street the surface has sufficient fall to give perfect drainage. The streets are unpaved except Johnson Lane which is full of ashes and filth.

'The yards on the north of the Wicker are generally close and badly ventilated; there are two which present an arrangement of houses over privies. In Dobson's yard one privy is frequented by 19 families and by the children of a school built over it. The privy is filthy and drains into adjoining houses.

'There is a yard in Snow Hill Lane where filth has been accumulating for years and is now heaped up to a considerable height above the level of the houses adjoining; this is not emptied for the narrow passage will not allow a barrow to enter. The adjoining yard is worse as the refuse is heaped upon the roof of one of these miserable dwellings.

'In Chequers Yard live some Irish families who gain a living by hawking matches, firewood, door mats etc. and who have scarcely any furniture and in many instances not a mat to lie on.

'In large numbers of streets tenanted by the humblest classes the house and yard accumulation is so imperfect, as to have originated a practice, much to be condemned, of throwing every kind of refuse, waste, food etc into the highway at all times of the year.'

It is not surprising that the conditions that have been described led to outbreaks of disease. One of the worst was in 1832 when an outbreak of *cholera* killed off many hundreds of people in the town. Streets were cleaned in the following way: 'It is the practice to scrape mud to the sides of the causeways and leaving the mud there for many days, weeks and even omitting to remove it altogether. It has been observed that day after day the same man has been occupied in rearranging the same mud into new heaps.'

This state of things arose partly because the town had grown so quickly that the two justices of the peace, who lived outside it, were unable to manage its affairs. Also the Overseers of the Poor and the Highways Board had no money left over to spend on improvements in housing and drainage or in fighting disease. Another problem was the increase in crime, which was the result of housing people under such dreadful conditions. 87

In 1810 the leading manufacturers of Sheffield made an attempt to get an Act of Parliament passed to appoint a body of officials whose duty it would be to light, watch and clean the streets, which were 'subject to various encroachments, obstructions, nuisances and annoyances and very incommodious and unsafe for travellers and passengers'. The Act gave Sheffield a body of men known as Improvement Commissioners who were given powers to carry out improvements to the town. They did attempt to light the streets with gas, but lamp posts were placed too far apart to be of real benefit.

At a time when Sheffield was growing and the town had no real government, the Church could have done a great deal to help but in Sheffield the Church had no interest in the working man. From 1754 until 1805 the vicar of Sheffield was James Wilkinson who was also a justice of peace and a squire who lived outside the town on his estate at Broomhall. You will have met this man before in 'The Agrarian Revolution'. Wilkinson had no respect for his church and although he was very generous with his money he had no time to help the men and women who were trying to solve many new problems of living.

The vicar of St Paul's, the only other church in Sheffield, was a very kind man but again he was not much help in times of trouble. Into this neglected town came John Wesley and at his first sermon the crowd threw stones at him. He wrote in his Journal: 'Hell from beneath was moved to oppose us. Those at Moorfields, Cardiff and Walsall were lambs to these.' When the mob pulled down two chapels which the Methodists had built, brick by brick, the authorities in Sheffield took no notice, but in the end the Methodists succeeded in building Norfolk Street Chapel by 1780. When Wesley visited Sheffield in 1788 he could write about 'the largest morning congregation I have seen in the Kingdom'. Success was followed by the building of Bridgehouses chapel in 1795 and Carver Street in 1805. The Church of England was late in providing additional room for worship. When after the Battle of Waterloo the government passed what was called the 'Million Act' to provide new churches only four were built in Sheffield. It was not until after 1840 that the problem was tackled in a serious way. If you look round your own district you may find some of the churches that were built under this Act and sometimes they are known as 'Waterloo Churches'. Do you know why they have this name?

Provision for education was not much better. There were only two schools before 1785. One of these was an ancient grammar school, off Townhead Street, and a boys' Charity School, founded in 1821. John Roebuck of the Carron Iron-works was educated in Sheffield and began the interest in science that became popular later in the century.

To provide education for the children of craftsmen, the Methodists opened a Sunday School in West Street in 1785 with the help of Daniel Hinchliffe, scissor-maker, Thomas Holy, button-maker and Henry Langden. Within five years there were 750 children in the Sunday Schools. In 1812 another school at Red Hill was opened for 1,200 children but this only touched a fraction of those who were receiving no education at all. A body of teachers and workers had also to be trained but by 1820 there were 11,000 children at school.

If you have read 'Learning and Teaching in Victorian Times' you will know that Joseph Lancaster was the founder of the British School system. He paid a visit to Sheffield in February 1809 and so impressed his audience that they bought an old rolling mill building and turned it into a school. The children were taught on a factory system of learning and in 1812 there were 640 boys in one room 89 feet long and 63 feet wide. All were under the control of a single master and groups of boys passed from monitor to monitor until they had learned their three R's, as they were called. In 1817 the National Society opened Carver Street School and in 1836 the Collegiate School opened in Eccleshall Road. A Wesleyan Grammar School was opened in 1837 but not one of these schools carried out what the founders expected.

The wage earners received some of their education through listening to Joseph Mather. He was a hungry *radical* who did not like hard work for low wages, so he earned a living by writing poems and reciting them in public houses. From time to time he was sent to the horrible little manorial prison in King Street, where men were sent for owing as little as sixpence. One of his best poems was on Watkinson and his thirteens which you have already met. In the riot of 1795, when the crowd supported the local volunteers who were demanding arrears of pay and Colonel Althorpe 'plunged with his horse among the unarmed defenceless people and wounded with his sword men, women and children *promiscuously*,' it was Joseph Mather who could sing, 'What the bloody tyrant meant, was murder without *precedent*.' He was not arrested for this and went round the pubs singing his songs, but the editor of the local paper. 'The Iris', was arrested and sent to York Castle for his report on the incident.

If you have read 'Parliamentary Elections and Reform', you will know that Sheffield was given the right to send one member to Parliament in 1832, so for the first time the growing town was represented. Another Act in 1834 had reformed the Poor Law. The Speenhamland System of 1795 had allowed overseers to make up wages of labourers by amounts which were related to the price of bread. This led to low wages being paid by employers, who were almost bankrupt, and so the hard working man had no advantage over the idle ones. After the Act of 1834, all persons wanting help must go into the workhouse and not receive help outside.

Two Boards of Guardians were set up to deal with the poor in Sheffield but the ratepayers objected to sharing the cost of keeping the poor with neighbouring villages. Samuel Roberts, champion of the poor, was shocked at the thought of people being driven into the huge bare workhouses, which reminded many of them of the stories their grandparents had told them about the Bastille in Paris in 1789, and so these workhouses were called bastilles. The Board of Guardians took no notice of objections and turned the old poor house into a new workhouse; before the end of the century these were to be a worse scandal than under the old system.

In 1835 an Act had been passed to reform the municipal corporations and enable new towns to apply for a charter to govern themselves. Sheffield was one of these towns and it was urgent that the three bodies governing the town should be united into one, for each left work for the other to do. There was a need for better policemen than the old watchmen, for in times of unemployment, hunger and drink drove people to riot. A petition was raised for a charter but so many people objected to the expense that it was refused. A serious incident in 1839 and 1840 caused the townsfold to change their minds.

The moderate men who had won the vote in 1832 were content to wait for further reforms to take place, but a body known as the *Chartists*, whom you will probably have read about, wanted more reforms straight away. They were planning to get these by violence and even revolution, as the French had done. Ebenezer Elliot composed a hymn to be sung at the Working Class Meeting in 1838. Here are three verses for you to read so that you can see what the people were asking for.

God of the Poor, shall labour eat?
Or drones alone find labour sweet?
Lo, they who call the earth their own,
Take all we have—and give a stone.

Yet bring not Thou on them the doom
That scourged the proud of ancient Rome,
Who stole for few the lands of all,
To make all life a funeral.

Yet not in vain Thy children call
On Thee if Thou art Lord of all;
And by thy work and by the word,
Hark, millions cry for justice Lord.

The Chartists attracted many followers in Sheffield and a great deal of unrest was caused. Only the firm hand of Sir

Charles Napier, the commander of the troops in the north, prevented serious riots taking place. It was the action of John Bland, chief constable of Rotherham that led to the arrest of the ringleader of the Sheffield Chartists, Samuel Holberry, while he was still in bed on the day set for seizure of control of Sheffield in 1840.

This led to two developments. The first was the setting up of a police force in 1840, composed of a police surveyor, his deputy, sixteen day policemen and fifty-six night watchmen. It was very hard to get men into the police force because the wages were lower than those of a steel or foundry worker. The second was another petition for a charter and this time on 31 August 1843 the town became a borough and could run its own affairs. So all the many branches of town government could be run from one centre and the tidying up of the town could begin, as the industrial leaders were given the task of setting up order and cleaning up the dark and dirty streets.

At the same time the colliery villages of Wombwell, Elsecar and Hoyland were expanding. Houses were built for miners on Hoyland Common and the village of Platts Common was growing up. In Barnsley the old untidy ways were to continue beyond our survey, for not until 1869 did Barnsley become a borough.

This illustration shows you how Sheffield had grown at the close of our story.

Sheffield in 1874

9 The Results of the Changes

The work of Richard Oastler, Robert Owen, Michael Sadler and Lord Shaftesbury had drawn the attention of people to the conditions of workers in factories. In 1833 came the first Factory Act which controlled the working hours of children and young persons, but even so many men had to work very long hours. So a further enquiry was held into the working conditions in factories other than textile ones and also into mines. In Sheffield a leading witness was Ebenezer Elliot who had this to say about workshops:

'The steel casting and converting shops are large and airy but the file cutting shops are bad. There are about twelve to twenty men crowded in a small room about four yards wide and three yards high. They are seated five feet apart and there is no ventilation. This causes tiredness and there are frequent journeys to the beershops for stimulant. Dry grinding is most unhealthy for the men breathe particles of dust, which eventually clogs the air passages to the lungs and causes the fatal disease known as grinders' asthma. The deaths occasioned by this disease are nearly one half of those under forty and carry off all before the age of fifty.'

The hours of work in the cutlery trade were shorter than in the textile mills. Cutlers rarely worked more than ten hours a day except when a rush of business caused these hours to be extended. When trade was good the workmen were idle on Monday and Tuesday but worked long hours for the rest of the week. Hafters' children, those who fixed handles on knives and forks, worked through a large part of Friday night and in this trade a fourteen hour day was usual. So you see that work 93 in the cutlery trade was very dangerous and men did not live long because there were no regulations about working conditions.

About half an hour was allowed for breakfast and tea, which was always called the 'drinking time', and one hour for a midday meal. The children left the factories for their meals except where water wheels were used and then all work had to be completed during the hours of daylight, for there were no means of lighting the small grinding shops. There were no opportunities for a wash or change of clothes such as we have today.

Dr Knight gave a description of the work of the grinder.

'He has to sit on a bench in front of a stone and on a level with it. He bends down and with elbows on his knees he presses whatever he grinds on the stone. He breathes dust from both and rarely lives above thirty-five years of age although a wet grinder may reach forty-five. They who are the greatest drinkers amongst the grinders are sometimes the longest lived owing to their frequent absences from work. [No doubt recovering from a bad headache after a day's heavy drinking.] The grinders usually began work at the age of fourteen, for younger than that they were not tall enough to sit properly in front of the grinding wheel.'

The cutlers' shops were generally airy, large, and protected from damp, but the grinding shops had their wheels too close together, so that the grinders were almost on top of each other. Accidents were caused by wheels breaking or the men getting fast in the driving belts. In any case grinders knew their lives were short and so lived a reckless driving life.

One apprentice said he believed that their love for beer was the main cause why grinders would not pay for flues to remove the dust in order to improve their health. They preferred to spend their money on drink. Another said that, 'anything which tended to lengthen the lives of the grinders would be disliked by themselves as tending to spoil the trade by enlarging the supply of labour'. The grinders thought that if they lived more than forty years the supply of labour would be more than the work demanded so there would be unemployment or else low wages and poverty.

The number of children who were ill-treated seems to have been much less than in the textile towns, probably because in Sheffield very few children were at work before the age of twelve. Out of six children who were twelve years of age and who were apprenticed to file cutters, four said they were well treated and did not find the work too hard, but two found it so tiring that they were unable to eat on Fridays. This hard labour made the children undersized for their age. There was also a complaint about the smoke: 'There are a quantity of small forges without high chimneys . . . one cannot be in the town for long without experiencing the necessary *inhalation* of soot which accumulates on the lungs. There are a number of persons who think the smoke is healthy.'

These working conditions affected the behaviour of youngsters. It was uncommon for the youth of Sheffield to attend church on Sundays and so we are told that 'vice is prevalent especially in the class who intervene between childhood and manhood and is aggravated at Sheffield by that system of letting out children to individual workmen whether apprenticed or not and rendering them independent of parental control at an age when it is most essentially needed. Both as regards habits, hours, education and religious instruction children are their own masters at twelve years of age, in general instances, throughout the industrial community. So Socialist ideas are rife in Sheffield.' This sounds familiar to us who are often told that children today are not controlled properly by their parents.

More people died in Sheffield from excessive drinking than in either Leeds or Manchester. In these two textile towns the steam power factories kept men continuously at work and, as one witness said, 'they don't know what St Monday and St Tuesday mean but here when trade is good they don't work for more than four days a week. As there are no set hours they leave work when they like.' You will not be surprised to find

95

Table 2—Class of Persons who were Apprehended

			Class of Persons Proceeded against on Indictment								
Known Thieves		Prostitutes	Vagrants, Tramps & others without visible means of Subsistence	Suspicious Characters		Habitual Drunkards (involved under proceedings held)		Previous good Character	Character unknown		Lo...
M.	F.	F.	M. F.	M.	F.	M. F.		M. F.	M. F.	M. F.	M.
52	11	32	1	"	28	3	4	4	111	26	20

Note.—The total number in this Table should correspond with the total number of persons as...

Table 3 (Table 4) Depredators, Offenders and Suspected Persons at la... and the Houses they...

				Number of Depredators, Offenders and Su...					
Known Thieves and Depredators				Receivers of Stolen Goods				Prostitutes		Suspected...
Under 16 Years		16 and above		Under 16 Years		16 and above		Under 16 Years	16 and above	Under 16 Years
M.	F.	M.	F.	M.	F.	M.	F.	F.	F.	M. F.
25	19	152	80			53	20	1	230	

Police crime sheet for Sheffield 1860. Notice the offences and ages of offenders

that half the people in beershops were youngsters under seventeen years of age, both boys and girls, and that some were only fourteen. No wonder there was so much petty crime. If you will now examine the police crime sheet you can work out for yourselves the ages of the offenders and their crimes.

Mr Abraham the churchwarden thought things were better in 1842 than they were in 1812, for in this latter year 'there was great trouble for the churchwardens in keeping the alehouses in order and the stocks were always full on Sundays, but there is less defacing of public buildings today and the worst offenders are the sixteen to nineteen year olds'. John Rodgers, whose works you can see on p. 98, said: 'Tuesday is a *natty* day with the grinders when nothing persuades them to work, not even a barrel of ale'. He thought that no child should be employed under the age of fourteen and

that they 'ought to be educated and have a certificate to show

Class of Persons proceeded against Summarily														
Known Thieves &c.	Prost-itutes	Vagrants Tramps & others without Visible means of subsistence &c.	Suspicious Characters		Habitual Drunkards (not under preceding Heads)		Previous good Character		Character still unknown		Total			
M. F.	F.	M. F.	M.	F.	M.	F.	M.	F.	M.	F.	M.	F.	M.	F.
...3 11	202	62 21	141	22	38	4	4	1	347	374	3785	855		

...te — The Total of this Table should correspond with the total number of persons proceeded against in Table 5.
...thin the District of the Police, in the Month of September
...ent

...d Persons at large				Number of Houses of Bad Character.							
Daily Average Number of Vagrants and Tramps				Total		Houses of Resort of the Police &c.	Resort of Thieves and Prostitutes				Total
Under 16 Years		16 and Above		Under 16 Years	16 Years & above		Public Houses	Beer Shops	Coffee Shops	Other Houses Junk Shops	Brothels and Houses of ill fame	Tramps' Lodging Houses	
M.	F.	M.	F.										
9	7	20	6	34 18	265 351	24	20	40	2		111	15	212

this'. Mr Rodgers was far in advance of his time for it was not until 1918 that fourteen became the school leaving age.

As usual it was Ebenezer Elliot who had the most important remarks to make about social conditions and he said that *hooliganism* and the poverty of the parents and the fact that education was not keeping up with the growing population was the root of the trouble. Hooligans roamed the streets at night tripping up pedestrians, especially the elderly. They are

'Wild ferocious gangs who compete in a narrow labour market in increasing numbers. After labouring in mill or shop from light to dark for six days in seven, neither children nor adults will seek the imprisonment of school or church—the only cure is a national system of education which should make ignorance a penal offence.'

But very few people were ready to advance in education as far as Ebenezer Elliot wanted and Sheffield had to wait until 1870

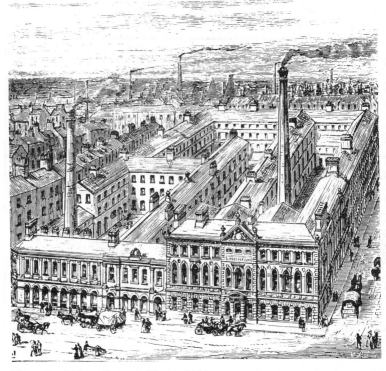

The works of Messrs Rogers and Sons in 1874

for state education.

Very different indeed were the conditions under which children were employed in the coal mines, remembering that Elsecar colliery was one of the exceptions to the general rule. Here is part of a report made by J. C. Symons for Parliament on some Yorkshire pits. As you read it I want you to notice the dreadful description of their work. The illustration is that of a girl miner described for you.

'One of the most disgusting sights I have ever seen was that of young females dressed like boys in trousers, crawling on all fours with belts round their waists and chains passing between their legs, in the pits at Hunshelf Bank and Holmfirth and New Mill. . . . I saw a girl of fourteen in boy's clothes picking down the coal in a place only two feet high.

Girl miner pushing tub

'On descending Messrs Hopwood's pit at Barnsley I found assembled round a fire a group of men, boys and girls; the girls and boys were stark naked down to the waist, their hair bound up under a tight cap and trousers supported by their hips. At Silkstone and Flockton they work in their shirts and trousers. . . . You have in the coal pits a nursery of vice which you will go far and wide above ground to equal.'

Girl miner

The result of this report was that Lord Shaftesbury was successful in getting the Mines Act passed in 1842. This forbade the
employment in mines of women and girls and also boys under
ten. Inspectors were appointed to see that the Act was carried
out.

Attempts were made to provide opportunities for working
people to receive some education, and though no single society
was really successful, they began a movement that was to grow
and become important. In 1804 Hall Overend started his
Society for the Promotion of Useful Knowledge. An advance
was made when Dr Arnold, the famous headmaster of Rugby,
visited the town in 1831. This is part of what he had to say:

'Our great manufacturing towns have risen solely with a
view to this relation of employers and employed. The very
name shows this that they are places where men have
assembled together, not for the purposes of social life, but
to make calicoes, hardware or broadcloth. A man sets up
a factory and wants hands; Sir, I beseech you to observe
the very expressions that are used for they are all signific-
ant. What he wants of his fellow creatures is the loan of
their hands; of their heads and hearts he thinks nothing.'

The importance of the 'hands' whom Arnold wanted to have
some other attention than hard work led to the foundation of
a 'Library for the use of Mechanics and Apprentices' in order
to 'satisfy the strong desire for indulging in the recreation of
useful reading at a time when the laborious classes can be
spared from their occupations'. This 'useful reading' did not
include any novels as these were thought to be unsuitable for
young apprentices. In 1832 the Mechanics Institute was
founded, and when employers objected to this because they
thought that it would make their workpeople restless if their
education was improved, it was said that 'there was no danger
that the increase of knowledge will cause those who possess it
to show want of respect to their superiors or to disobey their
masters. . . . The best and most orderly servants have invari-
ably been those that received the best education.'

100   The secretary of the Institute was Isaac Ironside and the

committee gave him the sack for allowing '*subversive* or chartist books in the library'. The Institute was followed by the founding of the Unitarian Adult School in 1842 and the Society of Friends School in 1845, but the most successful was the People's College founded in 1842 by the Rev. R. S. Bayley. This was the first college of its kind in the country and so popular was it that by 1850 it had 650 students attending it. Somehow all these efforts failed to give what was wanted. The working man was often tired out by the long hours of work and he had no training in the ways of study. Also the Mechanics Institute refused to buy the books which those people who were interested in politics wanted to read. So people had to wait for the opening of the Free Library in 1853 before they could get the books they wanted to read.

Many of the people who were concerned in this work were Christians but provision for religious worship was deplorable. The vicar of Sheffield said that before 1818 there were only 300 free seats in the church for a population of 16,000. A further 3,200 had been added by 1826 but only children used them so 'a population has grown up with no habit of Sunday observance and only one in ten attend church'.

The Wesleyan minister complained there were not enough schools so that half the children in Sheffield never went to school. He also said that teachers were badly paid and often bad at the job. Too many parents thought that they only needed to send children to Sunday School.

Opportunities for recreation were very limited. It is true that Sheffield society had the Assembly Rooms in Norfolk Street where they could dance and play cards, and there was a theatre at which Mrs Siddons, Charles Kemble and Edmund Kean performed. The workers attended and sat in the gallery or the 'gods' as it was called. They often made themselves heard and expressed their appreciation of the performance by throwing all kinds of things at the performers. But chances for outdoor sports were few. If you have read 'The Agrarian Revolution' you will know that Enclosure Acts had taken away the common land which had been used for cricket, football and horse racing. 'Scarce a foot of these common wastes remain for the enjoyment of the industrial classes.' To go into the cricket field meant paying a fee and the botanical gardens were only opened twice a year to the poor and closed on Sundays. John Wardle, a cutler, said: 'To the want of proper places for healthful recreation may be attributed the great increase in crime in this town and neighbourhood. Young people have no resort but the beer house or public house and generally those of the worst character.'

We must now consider what the people of Sheffield gained or lost by all the changes we have been describing. The first thing we must notice is that the Industrial Revolution changed the ways in which people earned their livings. There was a steady migration of people from rural areas into the towns and there were many Irish immigrants seeking employment in mining and other trades because wages tended to be higher than in the rural areas. After the battle of Waterloo there was a big increase in the growth of industry and also in the size of towns. Tiny villages and country towns grew into the modern Sheffield, Manchester, Bradford and Barnsley, which became centres of large populations. As people came from the country to the town, houses had to be built for them very quickly. There were no Town Planning Acts then and so back to back houses crowded together were soon built. These rapidly became slums, where life was very monotonous and dreary. Instead of teaching a boy a craft through an apprenticeship, which was also an education, he now learned one process only and many of his skills were never developed.

In the town, at the end of the day's work, there was nothing to do and no open field for a game of football or cricket. Many employers believed that the less enjoyment a working man had the better. So the magistrates tried to keep him from the amusements that more privileged people enjoyed. Where did they go? They went to the alehouse and later on amused themselves by tripping up and interfering with other citizens who were walking in the streets. The new town was not a place of beauty or leisure or colour but a place where families worked, ate and slept. Many members of Parliament were only interested in making a man a good servant, 'in laborious employment to which his rank in society had destined him'. At the end of the first Industrial Revolution men were in danger of becoming slaves in the factory.

There is another side to this picture. Life in the country was not always one of happiness, although country people were often healthier than those who lived in the towns. Village society was often under the strict control of the squire and parson so that when these people went to live in the town they found themselves without a leader. Soon they learned how to organise themselves into trade unions for their protection and, encouraged by such men as Oastler, Wilberforce, Shaftesbury and Owen they took an interest in politics. It was not long before they began to have ideas that wealth should be shared out better and that they should be educated like the wealthy folks. As the century advanced the worker began to get greater wealth and buy things he once would not have been able to afford. These people were the ones who pressed for reforms in politics and in social conditions. One important result of the Industrial Revolution was that we got the idea that life was a continual progress to better ways of living and this became the theme of the nineteenth century.

Change continues, and after 1860 there began the second Industrial Revolution from the discovery of electricity and new ways of making steel. Today we are in the third Industrial Revolution when automation, atomic power and new materials are changing our lives. When you pass through Sheffield on your way to Leeds think how this city grew up in most unfavourable conditions to be a leading one in the development of industry.

How Do We Know?

The information in this book has been collected from many sources. Some of this information was collected by travelling round the area with a map, and noting all the industrial remains that showed us what had been taking place in industry at the beginning of last century.

A study of the parish registers gave clues about the occupations of people who lived in the district and the accounts of the overseers of the poor gave us information about the state of trade and employment. A look at the houses showed us what kind of living accommodation was available for the working man of the period we have been studying.

The family papers from Wentworth Woodhouse, Cannon Hall and Noblethorpe Hall contain many letters about collieries, ironworks and other business interests. In many cases there are bills for goods bought or equipment provided for the works. An unknown map of a proposed canal was found in Lord Allendale's papers at Bretton Hall, Wakefield and this has been reproduced in this book.

Then there are the records of eyewitnesses like Samuel Roberts and Joseph Mather who described the life of the Sheffield they knew. The poems of Ebenezer Elliott give vivid descriptions of industrial life of the 1830s. There are the reports made to Parliament about working conditions in mines and factories. The local newspapers record some vivid accounts of events such as colliery explosions. Many industrial firms have written up the history of their works but there is still a great deal to find out about this period. I hope this book will encourage some of you to begin to search for information upon the industrial changes in England that affected the lives of everyone. You may find some valuable material.

Things to Do

1. Imagine you are a person living in Sheffield during the 1830s. Describe the street where you live and the way in which you spend your days.
2. Try to obtain a copy of the Parliamentary Report of 1842 on your own town and see what conditions were like then.
3. If you live in Yorkshire, try to arrange a visit to one of the museums where there are displays of early iron making and coal mining, e.g. Tolson Memorial Museum, Huddersfield or Leeds City Museum or Cusworth Hall, Doncaster.
4. Describe the life of a coal miner at this period.
5. Imagine you are beginning work at Walker's ironworks in 1785. Describe the changes you have seen during your apprenticeship.
6. Try to obtain copies of the parish registers for your town or village and discover the changes in occupations that took place between 1780 and 1850.
7. Try to arrange a visit to an ironworks or a steel works and see how different are the methods of manufacture today.
8. Write a letter to a friend describing the building and working of the Fire Engine at Elsecar colliery.
9. Write a report to a newspaper of the meeting of miners at Wakefield when they were forming a union.
10. You are an elderly person living in Elsecar. Describe the changes you have seen in the mining of coal.

Glossary

to abscond, to run away secretly

adit, mine passage cut horizontally into a hillside

to amputate, to cut off

annuity, sum of money payable every year

asthma, acute shortage of breath or difficulty in breathing

bannisters, cone-shaped wicker baskets for carrying charcoal

bargees, barge men

bell pits, early mines which were shaped like a bell inside

blister steel, kind of steel so called from its lumpy surface

bloom, iron hammered or squeezed into a thick bar

bloomery, place where reheated pig iron was hammered into billets

cages, iron structures used as lifts in a mine shaft

calcine, to burn out impurities

cavity, hole

cementation, changing iron into blister steel by heating with charcoal

chafery, forge in which iron is hammered into bars

Chartist, a member of the Chartist movement in 1839–1848

cholera, fever similar to typhoid

close, piece of land with a hedge or fence round it

colliers, men who burn wood into charcoal

combination, group of men combining together to get better working conditions

concourse, an assembly of people

contract, agreement between two or more persons for business purposes

cording, piling cut sections of trees into stacks for burning

corves, wooden tubs used for carrying coal down a mine

crinoline, very wide skirt held out by a frame

crucible, melting pot made of special clay

cutler, maker of knives and forks

datelors, men who are paid by the day
deposits, material left behind after water has drained away
deputy, a mine foreman
drawers, persons who pull tubs of coal
to economise, to use carefully
endowed, assisted by a gift of money
epithet, form of strong expression
to evince, to show
execrable, detestable
exorbitant, demand which is too high
feying, local term for removing material from one place, or clearing
   up the ground
fillers, men who fill tubs with coal in a pit
finery, place where iron is refined
finishers, men who carry out the final process in manufacture
fire damp, highly explosive and poisonous gas in mines
flux, substance which helps to clean metals
founders, men who prepare pig iron from the ore
fustian, coarse cotton or cotton and linen cloth
gin, shortened form of engine
goits, water courses for conveying water from a dam to a water wheel
gratis, free of charge
grindle cowks, worn out grindstones
hands, workmen
hangers on, men who join tubs of coal together by means of hooks
heading, beginning or end of a gallery or road in a mine
hearth, part of a furnace where molten iron collects
helve, water-driven forge hammer
hooliganism, violent attacks
hurrying, pushing tubs of coal from the face to the mine shaft
husbandman, farmer
inhalation, breathing in
latchin, local word for surveying
lathe, machine for turning wood and iron
law suit, dispute taken to a court of law
lease, period of years on which property is let to a tenant
load, an old fashioned measure of weight
malleable, iron which can be worked without breaking
measure (of coal), a series of rocks containing coal
mineral, an inorganic substance found in the earth like coal
mode, way, method
Naggs, 'nag' is slang for a small horse
natty, local term for day on which wages are made up

navigable, suitable for boats

nodules, small lumps of iron ore

Nonconformists, people who refuse to be members of the Church of England

outcrop, point where coal or iron seam comes to the surface

panier, side basket used for transport by pack horse

precedent, something which can serve as an example

promiscuously, mixed together in a disorderly way

puddling, removing of impurities from iron by stirring when molten

quartern, quarter of a pound weight

radical, person with advanced views on politics

refining, removing impurities

reprobate, wicked and depraved person

riddlers, men who sift charcoal in a sieve or riddle

royalties, profits paid to a landowner for permission to mine coal

sattle, local word for settlement

shallow, not very deep

sleck, very small coal

slipe, steel runner on the bottom of a tub

sloop, large barge

slump, period of very poor trade

to smelt, to extract metal from raw material by melting

sough, tunnel for draining water from a mine

spice, local word for sweets

subversive, corrupting

to teem, to pour liquid metal into a mould

tenter, man who looks after a steam engine

tinplate, steel plate coated with tin

trapper, one who opens and shuts doors in a mine

trek, journey

turning shop, room in factory where metal is shaped

turnpike, road on which a toll must be paid by travellers

upcast, mine shaft by which air ascends from a mine for purpose of ventilation

whimsey, steam winding engine

warrants, document giving power to arrest a person

water course, channel for conveying water from a water wheel